T0199159

Echoes of His Word

Thirty-One-Day Devotionals

JOYCE HENRICHSON

WestBow Press books may be ordered through booksellers or by contacting:

WestBow Press
A Division of Thomas Nelson & Zondervan
1663 Liberty Drive
Bloomington, IN 47403
www.westbowpress.com
1 (866) 928-1240

ISBN: 978-1-5127-2188-1 (sc)
ISBN: 978-1-5127-2187-4 (e)

Library of Congress Control Number: 2015919773

Print information available on the last page.

WestBow Press rev. date: 12/08/2015

Contents

Day 1: He Knows You and Loves You 1
Day 2: Let the Redeemed of the Lord Say So........ 6
Day 3: A Heart of Thanksgiving..........................12
Day 4: Preserver Through Trials.........................18
Day 5: Hold Your Peace 24
Day 6: Listen For His Voice 33
Day 7: Things Aren't Always As They Appear..... 39
Day 8: Hurry Up! 46
Day 9: The Throne of Your Heart.......................51
Day 10: Stand Up For Jesus 58
Day 11: The Power of Words 67
Day 12: The Pitfalls of Pride.................................75
Day 13: Spending Time With God 84
Day 14: Prayer 92
Day 15: Read God's Word...................................... 99
Day 16: Consecrate Do Not Deviate 105
Day 17: Stand Strong In the Lord 111
Day 18: A Rock On The Path 117
Day 19: The Truth and Nothing But The Truth ...124
Day 20: No Compromise 130
Day 21: Wake Up Before You Die 138

Day 22: Where Is Your Focus?.............................145
Day 23: Entitlement...152
Day 24: What Is Forever? 160
Day 25: Growing In Christ 168
Day 26: Are You His Friend? 177
Day 27: But God...183
Day 28: Judging Yourself Harshly........................189
Day 29: The Voice of A Thankful Heart 197
Day 30: Addicted to God 203
Day 31: God Understands 210

Introduction

We need to know and understand the Bible rather we are a minister or a layperson. We all need to have our minds renewed and guided by God's Word. Spiritual transformation starts in the mind and breaks down worldly thinking, and builds godly wisdom and character as we allow our thoughts to come inline with God's Word. As we continue to study the Word of God we will begin to see the world around us with our spiritual eyes and measure all things through the light of His Word.

To live a life as a victorious Christian we need to read God's Word on a daily bases. I recommend using a planned schedule to read through the Bible in one year. There are several schedules available though ministries on the internet, or you can set up one for yourself. But, whatever plan you choose, stick with it. Be consistent everyday in reading according to the schedule you choose. If you have never before read through all of the Bible, you will be amazed with all the facts, stories, and promises that you were not aware of which are contained in God's Word. You will feel the power of God's anointing as you dig deeper into the Truth of His Word.

Hoses 4:6 says, *"My people perish for the lack of knowledge."* The word *knowledge* here refers to knowing God's Word and His will and His ways. The best way to learn of His Word, His will and His ways is to diligently read the Word of God and become informed as you transform your thinking and renew your mind.

> *"And be not conformed to this world, but be transformed by the renewing of your mind, that you may prove what is that good and acceptable and perfect will of God." Romans 12:2*

We don't simply read about someone and really get to know them. We must also talk to them to truly know and understand them. We need to spend time with them and develop our understanding of their ways, their desires and their mannerism. It is the same way with God. God talks to us through the pages of His Word and through His Spirit speaking to ours; and we talk to God through prayer. The more we learn of Him, the more we are drawn by His Spirit to spend time with Him. Our love for Him will deepen as the treasures of His Word are revealed to us. Our commitment to develop a dedicated relationship with God has great benefits for now and for eternity.

My hope for this book is that it will help you to draw closer to God through a steady infilling of His Word into your heart and mind. Allow His Spirit to speak to you through the pages of His Word, that you may be transformed in your mind and spirit. This book was written for that purpose; to give you time to spend alone with God and focus on His Word. Each story contained in this devotional was inspired by the Holy Spirit. These messages were stirred in me to seek a deeper understanding of His Word. And my prayer is that it will stir you to do the same. I pray that your heart will be open to drawing closer to God as you read these devotions each day. To God be the glory!

> *"I will meditate on Your precepts, and contemplate Your ways. I will delight myself in Your statues; I will not forget Your word." Psalms 119:15-16*

DAY 1

He Knows You and Loves You

> *"For I am persuaded that neither death nor life, nor angels, nor principalities, nor powers, nor things present, nor things to come, nor height nor depth, nor any other created things, shall be able to separate us from the love of God which is in Christ Jesus our Lord."*
> Romans 8: 38-39

How reassuring to know nothing will ever separate us from God's love. God knows everything about you. He knows everything you say, think, feel and do. And He loves you anyway. There is nothing you can hide from Him. He knows all, and He hears all, and He still loves you. He knows your successes and your failures, your strengths and your weaknesses, and your joys and your sorrows. Throughout everything He is always by your side to tell you He loves you. This is all possible because, just as the scripture says, "*nothing can ever separate you from God's love.*" God knows all us and His love is eternally with us. No matter where we go, God is already there.

> *"O' Lord, You have seen me and known me, You know my sitting down and my rising up; You understand my thoughts afar off. You comprehend my path and my lying down, and are acquainted with all my ways. For there is not a word on my tongue, but behold, O Lord, You know it altogether. You have hedged me behind and before, and laid Your hand upon me. Such knowledge is too wonderful for me; it is high, I cannot attain it.*
>
> *Where can I go from Your Spirit? Or where can I flee from Your presence? If I ascend into Heaven, You are there; if I make my bed in hell, behold, You are there. If I take wings of the morning, and dwell in the uttermost parts of the sea, Even there Your hand shall lead me. If I say, "Surely the darkness shall fall on me." Indeed the darkness shall not hide from You, but the night shines as the day; the darkness and the light are both alike to You."* Psalms 139:1-12

There is no place where we can go that God is not already there with His love surrounding us. Under His mighty wings He protects us from all harm. When danger comes our way, God is with us. Even through troubling times He is at our side. He listens ever so intently to hear us call to Him. He swiftly brings us to safety as we place complete trust in Him.

> *"Though I walk in the midst of trouble, You will revive me; you stretch out Your hand against the wrath of my enemies, and Your right hand will save me."* Psalm 138:7

How blessed we are to have a god who we can call upon and He answers. There are no other gods who intervene on behalf of those who call on them. Our God is alive and active in our lives. If we listen to Him and follow His plan our security is established according to His promises. *"But whoever listens to me will dwell safely, and will be secure, without fear of evil."* Proverbs 1:33.

It is wise to learn of the God who loves us so much that He gave His only Son as a sacrifice for our sins. As human beings it is hard for us to wrap our mind around the greatness and power in such love. We cannot understand the depth of that kind of love. But, how blessed we are to be loved with a love that goes beyond description. God lavishes His overwhelming love on us even though He knows every detail of our life. Despite all our failures and imperfections, God still loves us. And if we have repented of our sins, He sees us as righteous.

We give praise to God for His love endures forever! Oh, what a merciful God who dwells among us and lives in us! Our God loves us no matter where we have been or what we have done. His mercy is new to us every morning. What a compassionate and faithful God we serve! Praise be to God our Father who knows all of our faults and He loves us anyway!

> "*Great is the Lord and greatly to be praised...*" Psalm 28:1

> "*God is our refuge and strength, a very present help in trouble.*" Psalm 46:1

> Heavenly Father,

> I praise You for Your love. Thank You for dwelling in my heart and for delivering me from harm. You know everything about me and yet You still love me. Thank You for a love that does not waver nor does it shun me because of the wrong things I have done. I choose to love You because You first loved me and You forgive all my sins through Jesus Christ. I am truly blessed that nothing

can ever separate me from Your love. Thank You that Your love is ever present. You have established me securely with Your everlasting love. What an honor to call You my Lord!

In Jesus' Name,
Amen

"The angel of the Lord encamps all around those who fear Him, and delivers them. Oh, taste and see that the Lord is good." Psalms 34: 7-8

"The Lord is near to those who have a broken heart, and have a contrite spirit." Psalm 34:18

"As the Father loved Me, I also have loved you; abide in My love. If you keep My commandments, you will abide in My love, just as I have kept My Father's commandments and abide in His love." John 15:9-10

DAY 2

Let the Redeemed of the Lord Say So

> *"Let the redeemed of the Lord say so, whom He has redeemed from the hand of the enemy."* Psalms 107:2

The day I surrendered my life to Christ I wanted to shout it from the rooftops. I was a six year old child when I accepted Jesus as my Savior, but it wasn't until I was thirteen that I understood what it meant to make Him Lord of my life. Once that I understood I needed to surrender to His will, and die to my flesh, it was easy for me to let God be the Lord of my life.

Ever since I was very young, not even old enough to attend school, my mother would do her household chores as she sang beautiful hymns. I loved basking in the peace that flooded my soul as those calming melodies permeated the very fiber of our home. To add to this, my two sisters and I at the tender ages three, five and six, attended Sunday school every Sunday morning where we learned of the sacrifice Jesus paid for our sins. The story of Jesus' love was confirmed by our grandfather every time he came from Missouri to visit us in Nebraska. As a pastor in a mission church in Kansas City, each time he came to see us he made sure to reaffirm to us the importance of having Jesus in our heart. We loved and respected our grandfather because of the kind and loving man he was. He had Jesus shining from his very being and I wanted to be just like him. I wanted the peace of God shining from my heart that I may have the opportunity to tell others of salvation through Jesus.

With these wonderful examples of Jesus' love portrayed before me at such an early age, it came easy for me to surrender my life to Christ and let Him be my Lord. Surrendering to Him gave me peace like I had never known before. As a newborn Christian when I was six, Jesus was my peace in times of trouble and He was my shelter from the storms of life. It is that "*peace of God which surpasses understanding*" (Philippians 4:7) that still continues to flood my soul.

> "*...and the peace of God which surpasses all understanding, will guard your heart and minds through Christ Jesus.*"
> Philippians 4:7

Though I didn't completely understand it at the time, I knew everyone should experience this peace and I was determined to tell them. It didn't take long for me to learn that my friends at school thought I was crazy and they didn't want to have anything to do with my God. I lost some friendships over my exuberance in sharing my faith. The experience taught me to wait for the Lord to reveal to whom I should share the good news of the gospel. Though I still wanted to shout it from the rooftops, I knew to be still and wait on God to bring about His plan. However, we do need to be exuberant for the Lord, but we must be lead by the Holy Spirit to know when to share the gospel and to whom to share it with. When we do this, He will give us the right words to say at the right time. But never stop telling of the love of the Lord and of His redemptive power.

If you have been redeemed by the blood of the lamb, you are to tell others. Don't hide it under a disguise of something the world finds more acceptable. Be honest and stand up for what you believe. We are to be a shining light in a dark world, but who can see our light if we hide it?

> "*You are the light of the world. A city that is set on a hill cannot be hidden. Nor do they light a lamp and put it under a basket, but on a lampstand, and it gives light to all who are in the house. Let your*

> *light so shine before men, that they may see your good works and glorify your Father in heaven."* Matthew 5:14-16

As redeemed born again believers, we should be so excited about our new life in Christ that we just can't stop talking about Him. We are to be a witness to all people through the kind of life we live and by the words we speak. Always remember you are a representation of Jesus to all who you come in contact with. God is love, and if we are not portraying love to others with our conduct and our words, why would they want to be a Christian like us? Live according to the standards God has set up for us in His Word.

We are the redeemed and we need to say so! Shout it from the rooftops! Our redeemer lives!

Being redeemed from the hand of the enemy means that God has forgiven our sins, He takes care of us, and He will keep us safe from the enemy. The Word of God says we are the "*head and not the tail; you shall be above only and not beneath*" (Deuteronomy 28:13), and we are "*more than conqueror through Him who loved us*" (Romans 8:37). God gave us the victory when he washed away our sins through the work of the cross. Now that is something worth shouting about! I am redeemed! What an awesome thing to know!

> *"These are Your servants, whom You have redeemed by Your great power, and by Your strong hand."* Nehemiah 1:10

> *"Yet I will exult in the Lord, I will rejoice in the God of my salvation."* Habakkuk 3:18 NAS

The word redeemed means reclaimed, recovered, buy back, purchase, ransom, reinstate, restore, and settle. Wow! That's what God offers us through the blood of His Son. We are ransomed from the curse of sin and reclaimed as a child of the Most High God.

> *"Christ has redeemed us from the curse of the law, having become a curse for us..."* Galatians 3:13

We have been bought with a price and the debt for our sin was settled at the cross. If this doesn't make you happy just thinking about what Christ has done for you, then you need to get alone with God and ask Him to bring back to your memory the moment you first made Jesus Lord of your life. Fall in love again with Jesus, the Savior of your soul. This is shouting news that should stir up the heart of every believer. If you have been redeemed you should say so!

Heavenly Father,

Thank You so much for sending Your Son Jesus. And thank You Jesus for redeeming me and giving me right standing with You as God the Father. It is through the ransom that You paid for my sins that I am now a new creation in Christ. I will continue to tell of Your mercy and love to all who will listen. I am the redeemed of the Lord and I will say so. Let my light shine bright to everyone everywhere. Help me to be bold in sharing the good news of the gospel with others, and to follow the leading of the Holy Spirit in doing so.

In Jesus' Name
Amen

"O Lord, You have pleaded the case for my soul: You have redeemed my life." Lamentations 3:58

"But let all those rejoice who put their trust in You; Let them ever shout for joy, because You defend them; let those also who love Your name be joyful in You. For You, O Lord, will bless the righteous; with favor You will surround him as with a shield." Psalm 5:11-12

DAY 3

A Heart of Thanksgiving

> *"Enter into His gates with thanksgiving, And into His courts with praise."* Psalms 100:4

As a young married couple with children, we lived in our hometown close to schools, shopping, and church. Though our hearts yearned to live in the country, we were thankful for the nice home God had provided for us. Our little home was a two bedroom and rather small for our family of six but it was the first home we were able to purchase. During the first eleven years of our marriage we had rented apartments or houses. So, with the purchase of our first home we were both very happy to have a place we could call our own. We were unable to buy a home in the country for the amount of money we had available to secure a home at that time, yet I continued to pray for a large country home where we could raise our children. I had faith that God would give me the desires of my heart because the Bible says He will (Psalms 37:4), and I know the Word of God is true. I also knew that I needed to be thankful for what I had before I could receive something I believed for. I was thankful for our little house and was careful to express my appreciation to God for it every day.

After six years of living in our small home my prayers were answered for a home in the country. The farm house was located only two miles from town on a paved road. The house had two stories with a basement and four bedrooms which sat on five and a half acres of land. There were five outbuildings and a double car garage. It had way more space than we had ever dreamed of having. God worked out all the details and before we knew it, the property was ours.

Moving day was exciting for our family. The children explored the many buildings and found small treasures left behind from families who had lived there before. It didn't take long to get accustomed to country living. The children enjoyed riding their bikes on our property, playing baseball and discovering new places to play each day. We soon acquired a farm dog we named Bumper, a dozen chickens, six ducks, two geese, ten rabbits, and two cats named Kodo and Podo. Along with acquiring our small animals came a list of daily chores to be done. The children learned how to take care of the animals which instilled good work ethics in them. The country life suited our family well. It was in this farmhouse where each of our children grew up, graduated from high school, went into the working world, and got married. Soon grandchildren were enjoying the farm just like their parents had.

Through the years as we lived in the farmhouse my heart was grateful for everything God had blessed us with. The peace and joy I received from so many blessings drew me closer to my Lord. I found a deeper hunger to know more of God. The Scriptures began to come alive to me as I daily fed on the wisdom in His Word. The more I studied God's Word the greater the gratitude filled my heart for Him and His mercy towards me. I began every day thanking God for His abundant blessings both great and small. Tears would flow from my eyes as I thought of the many provisions we so easily take for granted. I began thanking God for the light switches which produced light at the flip of our fingers. I thanked Him for our appliances that made life much easier and better for our family. I thanked God for our furniture that made life comfortable. I thanked God for our food and that we had the privilege to go into our kitchen, when we were hungry, and find something good to eat. I thanked God for our pets, the farm animals, and for our home and land. For the quietness of the country and for the space to enjoy life with our children. I thanked God for healthy and happy children, and for a hard working loving husband who was devoted to his family. There were so many things to be thankful for and nothing was too small to praise Him for.

It was through this overwhelming heart of gratitude that God showed me His boundless love. All the blessings we were enjoying were a gift from His love towards us. Even when difficult times came, I found God's love guiding us through the darkness and into His light once again. We know we can depend on Him because He always abides with us and He promises that He will never leave us.

The farm blessed our family in many ways and we were privileged to have lived there for fourteen years. Many memories were made in that old house. Memories that we and our grown children cherish yet today. After the kids were grown, we downsized and bought a ranch style home on two acres that was just the right size for my husband and I and our three little dogs.

As I think about that farm house today, I can see how God had taught me to be a positive person while He showed me how to live with a heart of thanksgiving. No matter what comes our way, if we can find even the smallest thing to be thankful for, then God has something to work with to bring us the blessings we are praying to receive. Life isn't always easy, but a thankful heart allows God to bless us even in the midst of a storm. A complaining spirit will block God's blessings, but a thankful heart leans on the promises of God which confesses His love and protection over us in all situations. And Oh, how sweet it is to have God answer our prayers and bring us out of a difficult situation! He does it with joy because of His great love for us.

> *"O' taste and see that the Lord is good, blessed is the man that trusts in Him."*
> Psalms 34:8

If you desire to move up in life and to be blessed by God's amazing love, then be thankful for where you are today. Thank Him for all that you have right now so that God has something to work with to answer your prayers. Learn to live with a heart of thanksgiving instead of a heart of complaining. Complaining keeps you stuck where you are and it will continue to bring you down. Cast off that complaining spirit and begin thanking God for everything great and small in your life. With a grateful attitude God will bless you in ways that you haven't even thought of. A heart of thanksgiving finds the good in all situations.

> *"In everything give thanks; for this is the will of God in Christ Jesus for you."*
> 1 Thessalonians 5:18

> Heavenly Father,
>
> I am so blessed to have Your Word to teach me the benefits of living with a

thankful heart. Forgive me for taking so many things for granted. Help me to remember to look for things to be thankful for in every situation. I will purposely live with a grateful attitude and express thanksgiving to You for the many blessings You have bestowed upon me. Thank You for Your love and mercy towards me as I learn and grow in Your wisdom and Your ways. And most of all, thank You for salvation through the blood of Jesus. I am blessed to be called your child.

In Jesus' Name
Amen

"*Oh, give thanks to God in heaven! For His mercy endures forever.*" Psalm 136:26

"*My lips shall utter praises, for You teach me Your statutes.*" Psalm 119:171

DAY 4

Preserver Through Trials

> *Many are the afflictions of the righteous, But the Lord delivers him out of them all.* Psalms 34:19 NKJ

God's Word has remained faithful throughout all generations and it will continue to be faithful through every trial you will ever face. Trust in God and see how great He is.

Throughout your trial speak this out loud; "I am not moved by what I feel, I am not moved by what I see, and I am not moved by what I hear. I am only moved by the Holy Spirit of God to do, and think, and say that which is in line with the Word of God. The Spirit of God moves me in perfect harmony with His will."

Trials come and trials go, but God's promises to His children remain the same. He says in His Word, *"I will never leave you or forsake you"* (Hebrews 13:5), and *"Jesus is the same yesterday, today and forever"*

(Hebrews 13:8). Since He never leaves us and He is always the same, we know He will always be at our side to bring us through victoriously as He has done for us in the past. His Word is true and reveals to us that we can trust in Him. Know your trials have not come to stay, but they came to pass, so let them and rest in Him.

Keep your mind on God and His promises to deliver you out of your trials. Stay away from thoughts of blaming, complaining, slander, doubt, backbiting and fear. They will cause you to get stuck and you will sink further away from the victory God has for you. Trials are only bumps in the road, they are not the end of the road. When we connect our mind with the mind of Christ we can learn from the trials in life and use them to bring us up to a higher level of serving Him. We are to *bring every thought captive to the obedience of God* (2 Corinthians 10:5b). He will keep us in peace as we travel through the journey of each trial with our eyes focused on His promises.

> *"Do not grumble against one another, brethren, Lest you be condemned."*
> James 5:9a

When we allow our flesh to rise up and blame others for our trials we hinder God from delivering us. He cannot, and will not, work on our behalf when we have hate in our heart.

Even if the trial we find ourselves in wasn't from our own doing, we must rise above it and not complain or put the blame on others. Be diligent to keep your eyes on God, your eyes on the Word, and your heart open to His direction. He will lead you and guide you through the trial. Yes, He leads us THROUGH our trials. He does not take us around our trials, or over them; but He takes us THROUGH them for the *'equipping of his saints for the work of ministry, for the edifying of the body of Christ'* (Ephesians 4:12) that we may mature in the fullness of Christ. We are His children and we are to walk in maturity through all circumstances. Each trial we go through in victory strengthens our faith and helps us to reach a higher level in His service.

> *"For we are His workmanship, created in Christ Jesus for good work, which God prepared beforehand that we should walk in them."* Ephesians 2:10

We are to hold the flesh down under the control of the spirit that dwells in us. The flesh wants to create chaos; the spirit wants to bring peace, wisdom and understanding. Chaos is the state of utter confusion and disorder. When you feel confusion come over you resist the devil who is stirring up chaos and turn away from the enemy. Turn towards God to calm your mind and bring you peace. Peace is the end of strife and the beginning of the state of harmony, tranquility, and serenity. Peace will silence the storm raging in your flesh and quiet your mind to hear God.

> *"And the peace of God, which surpasses all understanding, will guard your hearts and minds through Christ Jesus."* Philippians 4:7

Allowing God to handle your situation not only keeps you in peace but it also keeps you out of strife. When you handle your trials through your flesh, you open a door to the devil. Satan brings strife to destroy our life and it is one of Satan's main tools to cause division and death to a believer. Stay out of strife and away from the devil's schemes by keeping your focus on God's promises that He is with you through the storm. As a follower of Christ remember that God is for you, not against you. So stay on God's side and agree with Him.

> *"But when you do good and suffer, if you take it patiently, this is commendable before God."* 1 Peter 2:20b

We must also remember that when trials come into our life our attitude over the situation will determine the outcome, for better or for worse. The choice is ours to trust God and rest in Him or to reason out the situation on our own. When we completely rely on and trust in God we will not be moved by the flesh because of what we see, hear, or feel. We will only be moved by the Word of God in us. To deal with our trial in a godly manner we must keep a good attitude. We can't get into the blame game and we need to be careful with our words.

Read the Bible and rest in His amazing love knowing He will bring you through in victory as you keep your focus on Him; and the peace of God will keep your heart and mind on Christ Jesus and clear from dwelling on your situation.

> *"Humble yourselves in the sight of the Lord, and He will lift you up."* James 4:10

> Heavenly Father,

> Thank You for handling my trials for me as I turn them over to You. Remind me that You can handle it as I rest in Your peace. Help me to remember not to be moved by my feelings, or by what I hear or see. I rest in Your Spirit which dwells in me and moves me in perfect harmony with you. I am determined to keep a godly attitude as I go through trials that come my way. May each victory mature me to serve You with greater understanding of Your will and your ways.

> In Jesus' Name,
> Amen

"So then my beloved brethren, let every man be swift to hear, slow to speak, slow to wrath; for the wrath of man does not produce the righteousness of God." James 1:19-20

DAY 5

Hold Your Peace

> *"Cast your burden on the Lord, and He shall sustain you; He shall never permit the righteous to be moved." Psalms 55:22 NKJ*

Throughout the Word of God we are told to stay in peace. Whether we are experiencing times of blessings or times of trials, we are to stay in peace. During times of blessing it's not hard to stay in peace, but when we are faced with trials we need to put God's Word into action. How we react to a difficult situation reveals our true character. It is through these trials that we learn to hold our peace and hold tight to the promises of God. I had experienced a trial that threatened to steal my peace, but my faith and trust in God won instead of my flesh. This is a victory! Here is a recap of that situation.

I had waited several weeks for the shipment of my first completed book to arrive from the publisher.

The morning finally came when the delivery truck parked in front of our house and the driver walked to the front door with the box. I was so excited to receive my first book in print! I opened the box of fifty books and pulled out the one on top. Looking at it I said to myself, "I am now officially a published author." I thought of the long hours I spent writing each story, and of the many emails sent between myself and the publisher. Then I thought of the prayers, editing, more prayers, and more editing that went into creating the book, until finally we (the publisher, editor, graphic designer, and myself) all agreed that the book was finished.

As the printing began I anxiously waited to hold the completed book in my hands. Now here it was. I was holding the book and thanking God for taking me through the process successfully.

But something wasn't right. I felt it in my spirit, but I couldn't put my finger on what it was. I was happy, yes, but there was this uneasiness in my spirit. I remembered the past two nights as I lay on my bed just before going to sleep, I saw the book in my spirit and there was a flaw in it. Not a large noticeable flaw, but still there was something that needed to be corrected. In the eyes of my spirit it appeared the book was slightly curved in the middle, not completely flat. Both nights this same vision came to me and I knew

I would have to check the book over carefully when it arrived.

Now, with the book in my hands I thought about that possible flaw. I put the book on a flat surface to see if it was truly flat, and yes, it was flat. But still there was something holding me back from being in a hurry to get it distributed. I sent a picture of the book by phone text to my son in another state. He answered back saying the cover was beautiful, but he believes there was a word in the title of the book that was misspelled. I checked the spelling and my heart sank with disappointment. I was so excited to have my book completed that I hadn't noticed the error. He was right. The book was titled "Echoes of His Heart," but the second 'e' in the word echoes was missing. I didn't know when this mistake was made. I rechecked the graphics and the spelling of the front cover drawing I had sent to the publishing company to see if it was I who had left off the 'e'. I was relieved to learn it wasn't me. It was spelled correctly when I had sent the front cover drawing and title to the publishing company. Then I realized it didn't matter how it happened or who did it. What mattered was that I needed to get a reorder placed with the correct spelling so I would have good copies deliver to the bookstore as I had promised.

I knew in my spirit that I needed to keep my peace and allow this experience to be a learning opportunity. I knew if I kept my peace, that I could trust God to take care of the situation. The scripture in Romans 8:28 came to mind and played over and over in my head throughout the day. I gave the problem over to the Lord and I held onto my peace.

> *"And we know that all things work together for good to those who love God, to those who are called according to His purpose."* Romans 8:28 NKJ

I called the publisher to inform them of the problem. The lady who handles these situations was out of the office so I spoke with her assistant who told me she would have her boss call me back. After discussing my situation with the assistant I was concerned with the cost of correcting this error. I decided to trust God and wait on Him, instead of jumping to any conclusions. I simply needed to wait to hear what the publisher would say. I was also determined that no matter what the decision would be, that I was going to hold my peace, stay in faith, and trust God for a favorable outcome. The book I had just finished writing was about encouraging people to stand in faith, trust God, stay in His Word, and keep your peace; and I was determined to do just that.

All day I waited for the publisher to call back, but the call never came. I prayed about it again before I went to bed that night. I was sure God would work out everything for me if I simply stayed in peace. All night I kept repeating over and over in my mind Romans 8:28, *"And we know that all things work together for good to those who love God, to those who are called according to His purpose."* I stood on that scripture as I looked forward to seeing how God would work on my behalf.

During the twenty-four hours of waiting, (from the time I called the publisher with the discovery of the mistake until the publisher called me the next morning), my flesh was screaming inside of me. The flesh wanted to do something to resolve the situation. My flesh tried to plot and plan what to do next as the conversation I had with the assistant replayed over and over in my mind, but I refused my flesh from having it's way. I stood my ground as I stayed in faith, expecting God to work out the situation for me. Something inside of me said this is only a test and how I respond to this will speak volumes about who I really am. It will reveal my true character. When I heard this in my spirit, I was determined to keep my peace. As I held my peace I continued to recite Romans 8:28, my flesh finally quieted. I gave praise to God for His quiet assurance in my spirit and I slept peacefully through the night.

Early the next morning the publisher called me. She stated that they felt bad about the error in the spelling on the cover of the book. She stated that they would print my order again with the correction made to the spelling at no cost to me. Hallelujah! I was so pleased to hear her decision. I knew in my heart that this was the result of holding my peace and allowing God to work it out in His way according to my faith. I was pleased this publishing company had good integrity with honorable standards and was willing to make things right.

> "*...Be it done unto you according to your faith...*" Matthew 9:29

> "*In the multitude of anxieties within me, Your comforts delight my soul.*" Psalms 94:19

When going through a trial, we must stand on the Word of God and stay in peace. Don't fret or get into fear. It will steal your peace and drain away your faith in God's ability to bring you the victory. Stay in peace, speak words of faith and stand on the promises of God.

> "*Depart from evil and do good; Seek peace and pursue it.*" Psalms 34:14

Two weeks after my phone conversation with the publisher the correction was completed and my book arrived at my front door. A wave of peace came over me as I took the first book out of the box. There it was,

"Echoes of His Heart," with the correct spelling. It was as beautiful as I imagined it would be!

I praised God for teaching me throughout the process of producing that first book. God was the one who had stirred me to use the gift of writing He had instilled in me, and He had given me every word to write through the direction of the Holy Spirit. Since it was His idea, and since He wrote it, I knew He would bring the project to completion. I also knew He would get the book into the right hands to minister to those for whom it was written. It took obedience, perseverance, and faith on my part to complete the book. And through it all, I learned with greater understanding the importance of following the leading of the Holy Spirit, and I gained a lesson in holding my peace.

When we stay in peace, God can accomplish His purpose and His plan in any situation we are going through. It is when we place our complete trust in God and rest there, that we find the *peace that passes all understanding* (Philippians 4:7).

Do you have that kind of peace when a storm begins to form in your life? Can you feel the Spirit lead you in quiet surrender, or do you follow the flesh and cause more strife? The Word says, "*Blessed are all those who put their trust in Him*" Psalms 2:12b. So place your trust in God to lead you, walk in His blessings and see the wonderful results of holding your peace.

"And the peace of God, which surpasses all understanding, will guard your heart and minds through Christ Jesus." Philippians 4:7

"My brethren, count it all joy when you fall into various trials, knowing that the testing of your faith produces patience." James 1:2

Heavenly Father,

I ask for Your forgiveness when I lose my peace. Remind me when trouble comes, to quietly stand in faith and allow You to bring about Your purpose and plan through the situation. Thank You for the Holy Spirit who continually leads and guides me. Help me to remember to be still and follow His lead as You bring me the victory. Teach me through every situation I go through so that I may grow in Your wisdom and grace. I give You praise, for I know I can trust in You to bring me through to the other side in peace when I keep my peace.

In Jesus' Name,
Amen

"You are my hiding place; You shall preserve me from trouble; You shall surround me with songs of deliverance." Psalms 32:7

"I can do all things through Christ who strengthens me." Philippians 4:13

DAY 6

Listen For His Voice

> *"Incline your ear, and come to Me. Hear, and your soul shall live; And I shall make an everlasting covenant with you..."* Isaiah 55:3

Followers of Christ pray, read the Bible, and worship the Lord, but how many of us really listen to the voice of the Lord? When we read the Bible we need to have an open heart to receive what He is revealing to us in His Word. In Mark 9:23 Jesus tells us, *"If anyone has ears to hear, let him hear."* We listen with our ears when reading the Word out loud and when a minister of the gospel is delivering a message. And we listen to the voice of the Lord with our heart as He speaks to our spirit. To those who listen to the voice of the Lord, more spiritual truth will be given. A believer must be receptive and teachable in order to possess a healthy spiritual life and continue to learn and grow in godly wisdom.

> *"Listen carefully to Me, and eat what is good, and let your soul delight itself in abundance.* Isaiah 55:2b

The Lord tells us repeatedly in His Word to listen to Him and to tune our ears to hear His voice. Learn to pay attention to His voice and obey what he tells you. Some people say they don't hear God speak to them. Usually, this is because they are not listening with their whole heart. The world is full of distractions that pull our attention away from hearing God. If we want to hear the voice of the Lord speaking to our hearts, we must make it a priority to listen. Practice listening while you are in your quiet time with the Lord. Use your prayer time to not only talk to God, but also to listen for His voice speaking to your spirit.

> *"Draw near to God and He will draw near to you."* James 4:8

When we draw near to God we will recognize His voice when He speaks. Drawing near requires us to be still and listen. We must purposely make knowing God a priority in our lives. By doing this He will give us insight to understand His ways. It is in seeking the wisdom of God that we grow in spiritual knowledge and understanding. The scriptures say, *"Ask, and it will be given to you; seek and you will find, knock, and it will be opened to you"* (Matthew 7:7). And in

Deuteronomy 4:29 we are told when we "*... seek the Lord your God, and you will find Him if you seek him with all your heart and with all of your soul.*" In seeking Him, we must listen to Him, and receive what He has to say. One would not go to a wise man to seek his advice and not listen to him. In the same manner when we want wisdom and knowledge from God we must go to Him and listen to Him. Give Him your full attention. Be still and listen so that you may understand.

> "*For the Lord gives wisdom; from His mouth comes knowledge and understanding.*" Proverbs 2:6

> "*Listen, for I will speak of excellent things, And from the opening of my lips will come right things.*" Proverbs 8:6

The mouth of the Lord is His Word. He speaks to us through His written Word. He also speaks to our spirit in our mind and in our heart. Listening requires yielding to Him with our mind, heart, and spirit in tune with Him. Attend closely and wait attentively to take into consideration all the Lord has to say. When He has spoken, we are to receive and obey His directions. Each time we do this we take another step higher in our spiritual growth and understanding of His kingdom.

> *"Whoever listens to Me will dwell safely,*
> *And will be secure, without fear of evil."*
> Proverbs 1:33

To become wiser in the ways of God we need to seek Him, listen to Him, and obey Him. Why would we seek and not listen, or listen and not obey? It takes doing all three actions to learn and gain godly wisdom and understanding. But without purposely taking these actions, we will not spiritually grow or mature. We will remain stagnate and our faith will become stale. An active believer continually seeks the Lord for greater understanding. They constantly hunger for more of the Lord and steadily grow in godly wisdom. These are the people God can use to build His kingdom; those who seek Him and do not quit. Those who are perpetually seeking, listening and obeying are the faithful followers of God. They know the voice of God and they listen attentively. Learning the ways of God is a continuous process that, for the believer, never grows old. Those who listen to the heart of God will stand strong when the waves of trouble come and they will not be moved, for they are standing firmly on the solid rock of God.

> *"Get wisdom! Get understanding! Do not forget, nor turn away from the words of my mouth."* Proverbs 4:5

Do you desire to know more of God? Do you want to gain understanding and wisdom in spiritual matters? Then purpose to learn about Him by intently listening for His voice. Remember, when we draw near to God, He will draw near to us. But it all depends on us taking action first to draw near to Him. If we want to know Him better we need to make the first move. It's up to you to seek Him, hear Him, and then to obey Him. Seeking is the first step. Take that first step.

Listen and hear God speaking to your heart through the pages of His Word. Trust God to take you to a new level of understanding in spiritual matters. You will only grow according to how much you give of your time in seeking and listening to God. It is the law of sowing and reaping at work. God promises in His Word that, if we seek Him, we will find Him. In other words, if we listen with our whole heart, we will hear Him.

> *"Seek first the kingdom of God and His righteousness, and all these things shall be added to you."* Matthew 6:33

> Heavenly Father,
>
> Thank You for Your patience with me as I learn to listen for Your voice. As a believer, I am privileged to be able to hear Your voice speak to my spirit. Help me to not only seek You, but also to listen and obey You. I ask for wisdom

and understanding of Your will and Your ways, that I may walk worthy to be called Your child. As I read Your Word, help me to understand what You are revealing to me and help me apply it to my daily life. I choose to open my ears to hear Your voice as You direct my steps. Remind me that I will only reap according to what I have sown. When I give You my all, I will receive all that You have for me.

In Jesus' Name
Amen

"Hear, my children, the instruction of a father, And give attention to know understanding. For I give you good doctrine: do not forsake my law." Proverbs 4:1-2

"The entrance of Your words give light; It gives understanding to the simple." Psalm 119:130

"For where your treasure is, there your heart will be also." Matthew 6:21

"Hear, my son, and receive my sayings, And the years of your life will be many." Proverbs 4:10

DAY 7

Things Aren't Always As They Appear

"Rest in the Lord and wait patiently for Him, do not fret..." Psalms 37:7

While driving on the deserted highway towards home one afternoon, I caught a glimpse of a black and white furry animal in the ditch. Convinced it was a puppy someone had dumped off in the country, I decided to go back and check it out. Though I had driven a few hundred feet past it, I stopped my car and looked in the rear view mirror for any oncoming traffics. When I saw that the road was clear, I put my car in reverse and slowly backed up while cautiously watching in the rear view mirror. When I was a short distance from where I thought I saw the puppy, to my surprise, I saw two skunks cross the road behind me. I assumed it was a mother and her baby since one was much smaller than the other. I immediately stopped my car, shifted it into drive, and headed for home. As I drove away I thanked God for revealing to me what type of animal it was before I got to them and stepped out of the car. I laughed at myself for thinking I was going to rescue a puppy. If the skunks hadn't crossed the road when they did, I would have been the one that needed rescuing. Then I heard the quiet voice of the Lord speak into my spirit, "*Things aren't always as they appear.*"

Now whenever something in my life turns out to be totally different then what it *seemed to be* in the beginning, I think of those skunks again and what the Lord had said to me. Through the years, I have learned if I just wait on God to reveal the correct image to me, He will show me the reality of what had once disguised itself as something else. We must never get ahead of God by trying to figure out things on our own. What we think something is when we first see it, may not actually be what it really is. We need to be patient and allow God time to reveal the truth of the situation to us. Don't over think it! When we use our own understanding and reasoning instead of allowing God to reveal the truth to us, we will get ourselves into trouble. Patience can be difficult, but remember, the Bible tells us that patience is a virtue. According to Dictionary.com, a virtue is something that is morally right, and it is a good and admirable quality. Be patient while waiting on the Lord to reveal the truth of the situation. Be still, wait on Him, and stay in peace.

There are many stories in the Bible that end differently than what they first appeared to be. They are about people who waited on God to reveal His plan. Like in chapter eleven in the Book of Joshua; Israel, a mighty army of God, came against a fierce enemy who far out numbered the army of Israel's. If Israel had looked at the circumstances surrounding them, they would have felt defeated before they even started. But God told Joshua, *"Do not be afraid because of them, for tomorrow at this time I will deliver all of them slain before Israel..."* (Joshua 11:6). With full assurance and faith in God they boldly met their enemy and won the battle. It doesn't matter how hopeless the situation *seems to be,* God will give us the victory when we wait for His directions. Stay in faith and don't get into fear over the way things *appear to be.* Let God do His part and don't hinder Him with doubt and fear. When we judge the outcome by what things look like, we are defeated. Instead, we are to judge the outcome by God's promises to us. In Hebrews 13:5 He promises, *"I will never leave you or forsake you."*

In any and all circumstances, He is always there to guide and direct us if we ask for His help. If we ask to receive direction, but we don't obey God, we will still make our decision based on what we know, see, or feel. We cannot be guided by the Lord when we refuse to be obedient.

My first mistake was when I saw those small furry little critters in the ditch, I immediately felt compassion for a homeless puppy which was only existed in my mind. My second response was to say, "Oh Lord, let me help him." Though I didn't go through the proper steps of waiting for the information I needed, God was kind to me. He saw fit to have those little skunks walk across the highway right at the moment He needed to reveal the truth of the situation to me. "Whew! Thank you God!" When we act on what we think we know rather than waiting for God to direct us, we can find ourselves in a mess. And for me it would have been a stinky mess.

God has given us His Word to direct us and to keep us from harm, but if we don't know what is in His Word, we will get into trouble and then wonder why God allowed trouble to come our way. When things seem to be unclear to you, He will help you understand if you will only ask Him to give you understanding. It is by our ignorance, disobedience, or impatience that most of our troubles come. Our ignorance comes from not reading or knowing His Word, and by not seeking Him for answers or by being disobedient

> *"Ask and it shall be given you; seek and you shall find..."* Matthew 7:7

If I had taken the time to ask God what I should do, He may have told me to *"Be still, and know that I am God"* (Psalms 46:10). That would have reminded me to wait and listen for His direction before acting on what I thought I knew. It is so easy in the flesh to get ahead of God. The hard part is learning to discipline ourselves to seek God's input before we act on what things *seem to be.* Anytime we are unsure of something we are facing, we simply need to ask God to reveal the truth to us. He will help us sort it out so we will know the reality of the situation. It is the enemy of our soul who wants to hide the truth in hopes of trapping us. But if you know the Word of God and you incline your ear to hear the voice of the Lord, He will disclose to you what the enemy is trying to hide.

> "... *your adversary the devil walks about like a roaring lion, seeking whom he may devour."* I Peter 5:8

Stay in the Word of God to keep alert to the devil's plans. Then the devil will not be able to fool you into thinking something is other then what it really is.

> *"Therefore submit to God. Resist the devil and he will flee from you. Draw near to God and he will draw near to you."* James 4:7-8a

When we draw near to God, we will recognize His voice as He speaks to us. He will help us understand the truth of any situation in our life.

> *"In all your ways acknowledge Him and He will direct your path."* Proverbs 3:6

Do you have trouble waiting on God? Are you quick to act before you ask God for direction? Has the devil ever gotten the best of you by making you think something is what it really isn't? Do you want to know the truth in every situation you encounter?

If you answered yes to any of these questions, let me encourage you to train yourself to sit quietly before God everyday and listen for His voice. When you seek Him with your whole heart, you will find Him. He speaks to our spirit with thoughts that will always line up with His Word. As you practice listening, you will soon become familiar with His voice. This will help when you find yourself in a situation and you need His direction quickly. He will speak in a way so that you can understand what your next move needs to be. He will protect you and keep you safe as you follow His lead. Always remember to slow down and ask God to reveal the truth when you have a sense that things may not really be what they *appear to be.* Don't get caught in a stinky mess because you hadn't inquired of the Lord for Him to reveal what the reality of the situation really is.

> *"...you do not have because you do not ask."* James 4:3

Heavenly Father,

I come to You today and ask You to forgive me for not waiting for Your guidance before I make a decision. I thank You that You are ready and willing to help me if I will only ask. Help me to recognize when the devil has set a trap for me. Keep me alert to his plans as I diligently stay in Your Word and seek to hear Your voice speaking to me. Thank You for Your protection as I submit myself to You, and as I resist the devil.

In Jesus' Name
Amen

"But the Lord is faithful, who will establish you and guard you from the evil one." 2 Thessalonians 3:3

"Refuse foolish and ignorant speculations..." 2 Timothy 2:23

"But those who listen to me will dwell safely, And will be secure, without fear." Proverbs 1:33

DAY 8

Hurry Up!

> *"But those who wait on the Lord shall renew their strength; They shall mount up with wings like eagles, they shall run and not be weary, They shall walk and not faint."* Isaiah 40:31

How many times have you heard your child say, "Hurry up"? Children are impatient and they want to hurry in almost everything. They want us to hurry up and decide if the answer is yes or no. "Hurry up, Mom, I'm ready to go to my friend's house," or they may say, "Hurry up and pick me up right after school," or "Hurry up Dad, and decide if I can go with them."

Children are in a hurry to start school, to start the DVD player to watch the movie, to have a snack, to have their next birthday, to go to the next grade, to get their driver's license, to start dating, to start college, to start a career, to get married, and to start a family.

Their life is continually looking for the next event. But aren't we as adults just like them?

Hurry, hurry! We live in a fast paced world of hurrying. People are in a hurry to do everything and to do it quickly so they can get to the next thing on their schedule. It is like driving through thick traffic with many traffic lights. When the light turns green everyone rushes to the next red light and they wait. We get in a hurry to get to the next thing God has for us and then we find ourselves waiting to hear from God. If we would listen to God first, we would see He uses the waiting time to speak into our spirit that which we need to know to arrive at our destination safely.

It would benefit everyone to learn to sit quietly and wait. Waiting is becoming a forgotten practice. It is in the waiting that God can teach us. When we wait, we need to turn off our busy mind and focus on God. Let Him help you quiet your mind and unplug from the worries and troubles of the day. This is how we listen to God speaking to our spirit. I have heard people say that God doesn't talk to them. It is not that God doesn't talk to them, it may be they don't quiet themselves long enough to listen for His voice. He is speaking. The question is, are you listening?

> *"Be still, and know that I am God;..."*
> Psalm 46:10a

We often try to hurry God to answer our prayers. We are like our little children wanting the answer now. But like we teach our children to wait, God is teaching us to wait. Waiting patiently for God to answer our prayers demonstrates our trust in Him. We need to remember God's timing is perfect! He is the time keeper and He will do what He knows best for us when the time is right.

Our rushing around causes unnecessary stress. Pushing ourselves to the extreme is not good for our health and it takes away our peace. We need to slow down, unwind, and receive the peace God has for us. One thing to keep in mind is that hurrying produces less than the best. When we slow down to do things right, we will accomplish more than we could have if we had hurried through it. Let the quietness of serving God be your peace and strength.

> *"But they who wait on the Lord shall renew their strength..."* (Isaiah 40:31).

Abandon the hurried lifestyle and receive the assurance in your spirit that God will lead you as you allow Him to direct your path. God leads you in the path of righteousness, not by living in hurried chaos, but in steadfast peace and confidence in Him.

> *"Therefore the Lord will wait, that He may be gracious to you; And therefore He will be exalted, that He may have*

> *mercy on you. For the Lord is a God of justice; Blessed are all those who wait for him."* Psalm 30:18

Have you been hurrying through life? Does time seem to fly by and, yet, you don't seem to be making headway? Do you take time to sit quietly before the Lord and listen for His voice?

I had worked in several nursing centers, and the one thing most of the residents regret is that they did not take time to slow down and enjoy the life God gave them.

Determine today that you will not be living in regret someday because you lived your life in a hurry today. Allow God the quiet time He wants with you. It is in private tranquility sitting before the Lord where He will reveal His plans for you. Maybe it is time you change your motto from 'Hurry Up' to 'Slow Down.'

> *"And now, Lord, what do I wait for? My hope is in You."* Psalm 39:7

> Heavenly Father,
>
> Teach me how to wait quietly before You. Remind me as I go through my daily activities to set aside time to spend with You. Help me to slow down and appreciate the life You have given me.

Give me peace as I practice listening for Your voice. Show me Your way that I may walk according to Your purpose and plan for my life. Thank You for the peace You give me when I wait on You.

In Jesus' Name
Amen

"*When I remember You on my bed, I meditate on You in the night watches. Because You have been my help, Therefore in the shadow of Your wings I will rejoice.*" Psalms 63:6-7

DAY 9

The Throne of Your Heart

> *Then Jesus said to His disciples,"If anyone desires to come after Me, let him deny himself and take up his cross, and follow Me. For whoever desires to save his life will lose it, but whoever loses his life for My sake will find it."* Matthew 16:24-25

What is the most important thing in your life? Is it your children, your spouse, your home, your job, your nice car, or your status in the community? Is God anywhere close to the top of your list? I know this sounds a little harsh, but that is the question that God is asking us. He wants to know where you place the importance of Him in your life. Is He first place in your heart, or someplace farther down the list? Or maybe He's not on your list at all.

Who, or what, reigns on the throne of your heart is an important factor in determining what your life becomes. Are there things on the throne of your heart, or is God there? We need to ask ourselves that question often and continually check to be sure we aren't allowing anything to dethrone God or to take His place. We are to worship the creator, not the creation. If God is not first place in your life then you will go in circles trying to find something to fill that void. Nothing is able to fill a void that was created for God, except God. It is a God-shaped and God- size void.

Can you truly say, 'God is my everything and He is my inheritance'? When you allow God to be the one who supplies all of your needs, then you will have the greatest treasure of all. Earthly possessions only bring temporary happiness, but to have the One who is the source of all good treasures on the throne of your heart, is to have eternal peace.

> *"For where your treasure is, there your heart will be also."* Luke 12:34

To let God reign in your heart, you need to put away all efforts to portray the appearance of power and wealth as a means to impress. Your focus must be on God who gives generously to all who seek Him. You need to acknowledge that He is the source of all good things.

We are to seek God and not things, then He will bless us when He is first place in our heart. He desires to fulfill, not only our needs, but also our wants. When we have unwavering faith in God as our source, He responds to our desires. He simply wants to know that He is number one in our life and that He reigns on the throne of our heart.

There is a void in every individual that cannot be satisfied by owning things. Things will only bring temporary pleasure, but they are not capable of filling that emptiness permanently. The fulfillment of God's plan for us is that we will someday live in our heavenly home with Him. That plan is based on a personal relationship with Jesus, not on earthly pleasures. An eternal void cannot be filled by anything other than an eternal God. We need *more of God* and less of things.

> *"And my God shall supply all your needs according to His riches in glory by Christ Jesus."* Philippians 4:19

God's love cannot be purchased. It is obtained by seeking the forgiveness of your sins. It is a free gift to all who ask. Once we have accepted His gift peace fills our heart. The craving for things we once had will be quenched as we allow the fresh water of His Word to fill us and His Spirit to lead us. However, if we continue to strive for things rather than the One who created all things, then we will spiritually die broken and empty with no hope of ever seeing our heavenly home. We can break the yoke of craving things by surrendering all our desires to God. Our reward will be our inheritance of the kingdom of God. When we continue the holy pursuit of God, self glory through the ownership of things will be defeated, and we will direct all glory to He who holds our heart. It is up to each of us to dethrone things from the place of honor in our heart by giving that throne to God. Daily our desire must be to have more of God. Actively striving for more of God will *keep* Him on the throne of our heart.

It is okay to own things as long as we never allow things to own us. Our ownership belongs to God alone. We are not to allow anything to ever take the place of God. If we surrender all things to Him, He will give us all things to enjoy. Everything, including gifts and talents, are loaned to us. Remember, it is God who gives all good things; so never let things be your god. When we allow things to be our god we are worshiping idols instead of the one true God. There is one God and He is the Father in Heaven, whose Son, Jesus Christ died on the cross and rose again, that we might be free from slavery to anything or anyone.

> *"For there is one God and one Mediator between God and men, the Man Jesus Christ, who gave Himself a ransom for all..."* 1 Timothy 2:5-6a

What is your greatest desire? What is most important to you, more things or more of God? Can you remove things from the throne of your heart and give that throne to God? To remove the desire for things, we need to become serious about surrendering everything to God. This will involve a painful death of the flesh which does not die easily.

Our determination must remain on the pursuit of more of God at all cost. No turning back. No self-pity. No pining for things of this world. Our eternal soul is on the auction block and we must make every effort to not sell out to earthly possessions. When we place God on the throne of our heart we are securing our eternity with Him. Seeking after things to be better than our neighbors makes us weary and frustrated, since there will always be more things we will want. Stop striving after wind! We will never acquire enough things to completely satisfy our fleshly desires.

> "*...all toil and skill comes from a man's envy of his neighbor. This is vanity and striving after wind.*" Ecclesiastes 4:4 ESV

Keep God as your main focus and remember *things* will not get you to Heaven. You will only secure the deed to your heavenly home through a personal relationship with Jesus Christ. Determine today to make it a priority in your life to die to the want of *things* and give God His rightful place on the throne of your heart.

> *"But seek first the kingdom of God and His righteousness, and all these things shall be added to you."* Matthew 6:33

Heavenly Father,

Forgive me for seeking things instead of seeking You the author of all things. Help me to die to the desire of owning material things. Today I choose to make You first place on the throne of my heart. I seek to receive all provisions in my life through You and not by selfish gain. Keep me from envying and lusting after worldly possessions. My focus is fixed on receiving the deed to my heavenly home through Jesus, my Lord and my Savior. I desire to be all You want me to be and to have all You have provided for me through a close relationship with You. As Your child I desire to bring You glory and keep You on the throne of my heart.

In Jesus' Name,
Amen

> *"Eye has not seen, nor ear heard, Nor have entered into the heart of man the*

things which God has prepared for those who love Him." 1 Corinthians 2:9

"I love those who seek me, and those who seek me diligently will find me." Proverbs 8:17

DAY 10

Stand Up For Jesus

> *"For I am not ashamed of the gospel, for it is the power of God for salvation to everyone who believes..."* Romans 1:16

A group of people sat around a table during a luncheon after a funeral. It was a very sad funeral that had left the look of hopelessness on many faces. The conversation at the table was shallow; well at least it seemed that way to me. They spoke of the many accomplishments the deceased man had achieved. They talked about his family and how much they loved him. The conversation turned to the wonderful peace he must be experiencing right now in Heaven. My heart ached when hearing that comment. I so hoped and prayed it was true. But the Scriptures say there is only one way to God the Father and that is through His Son Jesus. Those that do not receive Jesus as their Savior and Lord do not have an eternal home in heaven. *Jesus said to Him (Thomas), "I am the way, the truth, and the life. No man comes to the Father except through Me."* John 14:6

I knew that neither the deceased man, nor any of his family members professed to be Christians, and they did not live according to the Word of God. And from all the evidence we could see of his life there was no sign that he had ever repented of his sins. We do not judge, but we do discern. And what I discerned in my spirit was that this man had never given his heart to God, nor did he at any time confess to know Jesus as Lord. I hope and pray that he repented of his sins before he took his last breath. Only God knows for sure.

> *"...Truly, truly, I say to you, unless one is born again, he cannot see the kingdom of God..."* John 3:3

The Bible clearly tells us if we die without asking for forgiveness of our sins, then our soul will not go to heaven when we die. For the citizens of heaven are they who have washed their robes in the blood of the lamb. They are those who have confessed their sins to God and received Jesus as their Lord and Savior. Their life has been transformed out of darkness and into the light and they bear fruit of that new life in Christ.

> *"For our citizenship is in heaven, from which also we eagerly wait for a savior, the Lord Jesus Christ."* Philippians 3:20

> *"For this is the will of My Father, that everyone who beholds the Son and believes in Him, may have eternal life; and I Myself will raise him up on the last day."* John 6:40

A funeral is a time to help bring comfort and peace to those who grieve. It is not the time to point out the failures of the deceased. For the born again believer attending this type of funeral, it is a difficult situation to be in, but one which we often face. How do we speak up for Jesus at a funeral where we see so many who are spiritually dead? We simply love them as Jesus loves them. We don't love their sins, but we love them through Christ. How can we lead anyone to the Lord if we ourselves don't demonstrate His love through us?

Those lost in sin have no answers about eternity. They only hear what the world believes, and they accept it to be true. But, it is not the truth! The world does not have the answers. They say things like, "The Lord needed another angel in Heaven." Or they may say, "God called him home and now he is an angel in Heaven watching over us." **Wrong!** The world has it wrong! People need to read what the Word of God says and get their facts straight. People are people and angels are angels. If God wants more angels He will create them. And if He wants more people, He will create them. A person never becomes an angel.

Also, God does not call us home. We willingly give up our life. The Bible says, "*Death and life are in the power of the tongue*" (Proverbs 18:21). What you speak with your mouth is what will come into your life. When you speak words inline with Jesus, He will lift you up and give you a long abundant life. But when you speak words inline with Satan, he will tear you down and destroy you. A persons life that is cut short was not from God the Father in Heaven. It was from the god of this world, Satan. All good things come from God. All evil and harm comes from Satan, the god of this world. That's what the Bible says.

> "*For the wisdom of this world is foolishness to God.*" 1 Corinthians 3:19a

> "*The thief does not come except to steal, and to kill, and to destroy. I have come that they may have life, and that they may have it more abundantly.*" John 10:10

We have so much more information of the plan of God than the world could ever understand. For we who believe, know that only God's Word has the answers to our present life and to our eternal home. The souls of those who are born again in Christ are promoted to their heavenly home when they take their last breath on earth. We know without a doubt that we have eternal life with the Lord because we trust in the Word of God. Those loved ones we leave behind are not grieving as if there is no hope. If they too know Jesus as their Savior they know they will see us again when they leave this life on earth. So we rejoice, for our hope is in the Lord!

Some people say, "Why would a loving God send people to hell?" It is not God who sends them to hell, they themselves do it by their choice. We are given a free will to choose to serve God or to serve self, through Satan, the god of this world. The Bible tells us to choose life, which is to choose God our Heavenly Father.

> *"Therefore, whoever confesses Me before men, him I will also confess before My Father who is in heaven. But whoever denies Me before men, him will I also deny before My Father who is in heaven."* Matthew 10:32-33

It is our job as a follower of Christ to proclaim the salvation of the Lord in hopes of drawing non-believers out of the darkness. Jesus said in John 12:46, *"I have come as light into the world, that everyone who believes in Me may not remain in darkness."*

We who love and serve the Lord are to proclaim His love to all. But it is the choice of the unsaved to live in darkness even when they have been told of the light of Jesus that is available to them. We cannot, and would not, want to make them repent. It has to come from their free will. We do our job of ministering to the lost and we let the Holy Spirit do the drawing. Some people want to stay in the darkness, ' *...they love the approval of men more than the approval of God'* John 12:45.

But just because they desire their present dark state, it does not mean we are to stop proclaiming Jesus to them. Even if they won't listen to you simply live a godly life which will speak volumes to them about the loving God you serve. Jesus said, *"If I be lifted up from the earth, (I) will draw people to Myself"* John 12:32. We are the ones who are to lift Him up for the world to see.

> *"There is salvation in no one else; for there is no other name under heaven that has been given among men, by which we must be saved."* Acts 4:12

Don't live a life of regret for not speaking up for Jesus to those who have already left this earth. Determine in your heart to continually announce the saving grace of Jesus. Stand up for Jesus with your words and actions. Remember you may be the only Jesus some people may ever see. Which means the Jesus you reflect from your life may be all they will ever know of Him. Pray that by your example they will hunger for God and seek Him for themselves. As soon as a person accepts Jesus they can know without a doubt that they will be with the Lord in Heaven when they leave this world if they continue to stand strong in faith.

Paul, in the Bible, was forgiven of the sin of hunting down and killing Christians. He had repented and received forgiveness from the Lord; then he went out and proclaimed Jesus to others in hopes that they would repent of their sins too. We have the same reassurance of being forgiven. We were spiritually dead and are now spiritually alive through the blood of Jesus who washed away our sins.

> *"But now in Christ Jesus you who were once far off have been brought near by the blood of Christ."* Ephesians 2:13

We are to maintain a solid stance on the Word of God by telling the world Jesus still saves the lost and He heals the wounded. Stand up for Jesus in everything you say and do. Whether you are in the company of the saved or the unsaved, your words are to continually line up with the Word of God. Stand up for Jesus with acts of kindness throughout your day. In doing so, it will be evident to everyone that the love of God is established in you. There are many ways in which you can publicly illustrate God's love. Ask God every morning to manifest His love through you toward those whom you come in contact with. It will not only testify of God's love, but it may brighten the day of someone who is feeling discouraged. Let God work through you as you stand up for Jesus.

> *"For all the people walk each in the name of his god, but we will walk in the name of the Lord our God forever and ever."* Micah 4:5

Heavenly Father,

Help me to be bold in standing up for You and Your Word. You desire for all to be saved, that everyone may know they have a home in Heaven. Give me the words to say to share this wonderful promise with the lost. May my life always reveal Your love towards everyone in all I do and say. I am so thankful that I can stand up for Jesus because He had ransomed me from the penalty of death with His shed blood on the cross. Thank You for the victorious life You have given me.

In Jesus' Name,
Amen

"Let your gentleness be known to all men. The Lord is at hand." Philippians 4:5

"My righteous one shall live by faith; and if he shirks back, My soul has no pleasure in him. But we are not of those who shirk back to destruction, but of those who have faith to the preserving of the soul." Hebrews 10:38-39 NSA

DAY 11

The Power of Words

> *"Let your speech always be with grace, seasoned with salt, that you may know how you ought to answer each one."*
> Colossians 4:6

Did you ever notice when you dig a hole that there's not enough dirt to fill the hole back up? As the dirt settles back down it sinks lower than the ground around it, leaving a reminder that a hole had been there. Words are like that hole. Once spoken, they cannot be taken back. When the words are hurtful they can leave a scar in a relationship. Though apologies may be given, the negative words are still in your mind. We must always remember to stop and think before we speak because words spoken cannot be erased. Sometimes people may say, "I take it back." But negative hurtful words are not easily forgotten.

When words are spoken in court that could be harmful to the case, the defending attorney says,

"Your Honor, I object!" The judge then says, "The remarks will be stricken from the records." However, even though the remark is no longer on the record, it still remains in the minds of the jury. That's exactly why the prosecuting attorney said them. He knows the jury may be swayed by something that was said, even though it was supposed to be forgotten. He knows that words can be forgiven, but they are not forgotten.

> "*Let no corrupt word proceed out of your mouth, but what is good for necessary edification, that it may impart grace to the hearers.*" Ephesians 4:29

As a writer, one of the best gifts I can receive is a new tablet full of blank pages to be written on. I love filling new pages with creative words that were stuck in my head. A tablet full of clean paper allows me an opportunity to write out the thoughts that are on my mind. The written word can then be read over whenever we want to remember our past thoughts and ideas. Some people, like me, need to write down list to remember things. This is a good example of the written word being helpful. Words can be marvelous when they are helpful and used to encourage and are kind. When we hear or say the right words, we can be spiritually inspired or inspire others. When we hear sad or negative words, they produce the feeling of sadness and negative thoughts. They may even bring us to tears. Words can move us like nothing else can. Words can make or break us, and they have done so to all of us. The words we speak bring us success or failure. Nothing determines more how you feel each day than words do.

> *"Let the words of my mouth and the meditation of my heart be acceptable in Your sight, Oh Lord, my strength and my Redeemer."* Psalm 19:14

The Bible is called '*the living word*' because words are alive. They give life and they can take life. Words have great creative power to bring forth that which we speak. What we create with our words depends on the words we choose to say. This is true with God's words since they always produce that which He says. In the Word of God we are told there is power in the tongue (our words). *"Death and life are in the power of the tongue, And those who love it will eat its fruit"* Proverbs 18:21. This means what you say and believe is what you get.

Words cause things to happen or not to happen for us each day. Words are always in motion around us. Even when we are silent, words are continually playing over in our mind. Words can be kind and soft, or they can be loud and harsh. The order in which we put our words and the tone in which we deliver them will determine what others think about us.

Though we don't think of it often our words are building our future. Jesus said, "*But those things which proceed out of the mouth come from the heart, and they defile a man. For out of the heart proceed evil thoughts, murders, adulteries, fornication, thefts, false witness, blasphemies. These are the things which defile a man, but to eat with unwashed hands does not defile a man,"* Matthew 15:18-20. It is the words we speak that defile us.

Words can ruin our life when we choose to say things we should not be saying, or claim things over our life that we should not be claiming. For example, if you say, "I know I'll get the flu this winter because I always do." Then you give your body no choice but to allow the flu to come upon you. The words you spoke allowed an open door for the enemy to bring sickness to you, because you are speaking in agreement with the him. This is one of those times that we need to remember what the Bible says, "*You are snared by the words of your mouth*" Proverbs 6:2a. Instead of agreeing with the enemy, we are to claim health and healing over ourselves no matter what illnesses is going around. Say, "I will not get sick. I belong to the Lord and the enemy has no authority over me." Practice saying this in faith and remember that you will have what you say, whether it is good or bad.

Just like the hole that never seems to be completely filled, or the statement made in court that was asked to be forgotten, when words are spoken they stay in our mind. This is why we need to practice speaking words inline with the Word of God. God's Words are what we need to be meditating on.

> "*...Whatever things are true, whatever things are noble, whatever things are just, whatever things are pure, whatever things are lovely, whatever things are of good report, if there be any virtue and if there is anything praiseworthy – meditate on these things.*" Philippians 4:8

Speaking words of praise and thankfulness can calm your soul and bring about health to your body. Doctors have discovered that living thankful while speaking words of kindness can bring about healing. Positive words can calm the mind, lower blood pressure, reduce stress and inflammation, and improve blood flow. We must be careful choosing our words. If we keep in mind that our words have power to change our life, then we can train ourselves to speak with wisdom. We can also learn to keep our mouth shut when negative words come into our mind.

In the Bible, the book of Proverbs has much to say about the words we choose. It is good to read Proverbs daily to keep in mind how important our words are.

> *"There is one who speaks rashly like the thrust of a sword. But the tongue of the wise brings healing."* Proverbs 12:18

> *"Lying lips are an abomination (vile) to the Lord; But those who deal faithfully are His delight."* Proverbs 12:22

> *"The lips of the wise spread knowledge; But the heart of fools are not so."* Proverbs 15:7

> *"A man has joy by the answer of his mouth, And a word spoken in due season, how great it is!"* Proverbs 15:23

> *"A soft answer turns away wrath, but a harsh word stirs up anger."* Proverbs 15:1

> *"Whoever guards his mouth and tongue keeps his soul from trouble."* Proverbs 21:23

These are just a few examples of what the Word of God has to say about the words we speak. Search the scriptures to gain wisdom on how to use words to bring health, peace, and joy into your life and to those around you. Becoming wise in speech is learned through a lifetime of staying in the Word of God. We will always have room for improvement in how to speak correctly in each situation. As we read the Word, we train our mind about what to think on and how to talk. We will soon notice our speech is kind and full of knowledge and understanding. This is because the Word is transforming our mind to think and speak in agreement with God. When we speak in agreement with God we can use the power of our words to edify and lift up the name of Jesus. In doing so, we can minister with words of compassion to people hungry to hear the Word of God.

> *"And my speech and my preaching were not with persuasive words of human wisdom, but in demonstration of the Spirit and of power, that your faith should not be in the wisdom of men but in the power of God."* I Corinthians 2:4

Heavenly Father,

Thank You for Your Word which teaches me how to speak in agreement with You. I desire to learn to speak in agreement with You. I pray that that which I speak is sweet to Your ears. Help me to never talk with harsh words to anyone and remind me to be still before You to gain instruction to receive the right words to say. May my words never stir up trouble or cause others to be provoked. May my speech be with kindness and love in just the same manner that You speak to me. Help me to keep silent and not blurt out that which is not edifying to the hearer. Remind me that my words have power which can create or destroy. I desire to only speak that which is honorable and comes from a heart of love.

In Jesus' Name
Amen

"Out of the same mouth proceed blessings and cursing. My brethren, these things ought not to be so." James 3:10

"A good man out of the good treasures of his heart brings forth good things, and an evil man out of the evil treasure brings forth evil things. But I say to you that for every idle word men may speak, they will give account of it in the day of judgment. For by your words you will be justified, and by your words you will be condemned." Matthew 12:35-37

DAY 12

The Pitfalls of Pride

> *"Pride goes before destruction, And a haughty spirit before a fall."* Proverbs 16:18

To help us understand pride we will first need to know a few facts about pride. Here is a list of some of the characteristic of pride:

- Pride is boastful and arrogant.
- Pride says, "My opinion is the only one that matters and everyone else is wrong."
- Pride is selfish.
- Pride sees no wrong in sinning in order to get it's own way.
- Pride tears down others and brings about division.
- Pride says, "I worked hard, I deserve to be honored."
- Pride is quick to be offended or insulted.
- Pride takes everything personally.

- Pride is led by feelings.
- Pride always hungers for more recognition.
- Pride and boasting are empty of value.
- Pride got Satan kicked out of heaven

Don't take a chance of being kicked out of the kingdom of God by holding pride in your heart.

As a believer we may think those people who have a problem with pride are the unbelievers of this world. And, yes, they do have pride, but we also have pride. Believers aren't exempted from becoming puffed up with pride. For instance, we may be proud of our righteousness when actually it is not us who gives righteousness, but it is God. He gave us His righteousness when we gave our life to Him. Our righteousness is not of ourselves and therefore we cannot take credit for it. We certainly cannot be puffed up and prideful for something that was freely given to us.

> "*Whoever exalts himself will be humbled, and he who humbles himself will be exalted.*" Matthew 23:12

Pride comes in many forms. We are told in the secular world to have pride in our sports team, pride in our school, pride in our work and pride in our family. We are to take pride in our appearance, in our status in the community, in our success, our education, and pride in our charity towards others. But we are taught from the Bible that pride brings destruction. So what is pride and why does the world tell us to have pride while God's Word tells us not to have pride?

We have read the description of what pride does and how it acts. It showed us how holding pride in our heart is not a good thing. We can be pleased with things and praise God for them, but that is not having pride. It is having a grateful heart and appreciating the gifts God has blessed us with. Everything good that we have and everything good that we get is from God. He is the supplier of all things good. Without Him we would not even exist.

Hebrews 1:3 says that, "*...He upholds all things by the word of His power...*" We cannot rightfully have pride in the good things in our life since we did not earn them, they are all gifts from God.

Dictionary.com defines the word 'pride' as a high opinion of one's self dignity and importance. It is a state of being proud and a sense of what is due to oneself or position. It is ego, gratification, self-admiration, self-glorification, self-love, and self-worth.

Reading through this list we can see that this is not the attitude God's people are suppose to have. Pride is full of self. It elevates oneself above others. We are never to put the emphasis on ourselves. It creates selfishness and that is not how a true follower of God is to act.

> *"The fear of the Lord is to hate evil; Pride and arrogance and the evil way and the perverse mouth I hate."* Proverbs 8:13

Pride has everything backwards. It takes credit for what God gives and rewards the receiver instead of the giver. Pride turns the focus inward with praise of self instead of outward with praise to God. When we focus on self pride will lead us to destruction (Proverbs 16:18). If we take credit for God's goodness we are setting ourselves up for failure. God's protection over us is hindered from our selfish pride and we will eventually get caught in our own trap.

> *"Everyone proud in heart is an abomination to the Lord; though they join forces, none will go unpunished."* Proverbs 16:5.

God attempts to get their attention, but when the prideful person doesn't turn from their conceit and repent, then calamity falls upon him. *"The wicked in his pride persecutes the poor; let them be caught in the plots which they have devised,"* (Psalms 10:2). This scripture tells us to be humble and repent of pride or it will destroyed us.

Pride says, "I have no pride." It is a prideful thing to boast that we have no pride. It is just like the sinner saying I have no sin. Pride also says, "I can do it on my own," even if we don't know how to do something. We need to admit when we don't know something. The problem is not in the not knowing, it is in not wanting to admit we don't know. It can come from the fear of judgment from others that makes us want to cover up what we don't know. That is pride. God cannot use us when we are full of pride. We don't mature in a godly manner when our attention is focused on ourselves.

> "*Woe to those who are wise in their own eyes, And prudent in their own sight.*"
> Isaiah 5:21

Pride is a worldly sin and is passed on to each generation through those who live with worldly thinking. The world belongs to the devil who gained the rights to it from Adam when he disobeyed God. Those who follow Satan think and act in a worldly manner. Not only do they live with pride in their life, but they encourage others to have pride in many worldly opinions and ideas. But, God says, as believers, we are to be in the world but not of the world. We are to be set apart by our righteousness. If we are living righteously we will be alert to the sin of pride and not accept it into our way of life.

Pride takes away blessings that were meant to be ours. We cannot walk in the full blessings of God when we are full of pride. We must humble ourselves under the mighty hand of God that He may strip us from the arrogance of pride. When we humbly give ourselves to God, He will lift us up and show us His mercy. Check your attitude often to make sure you aren't being prideful in any area of your life.

Some things to remember about pride are:

- Pride never gives up and it never stops being selfish.
- Pride lacks generosity and is slow to have compassion and understanding.
- Pride finds fault and condemns others while looking out only for itself.
- Pride refuses to admit failures. It hides the truth and lies to cover up the truth.
- The prideful person holds hate, envy and jealousy in his heart.

If we see any of these traits rise up in us, we need to humble ourselves before God and repent. It is time to die to selfish pride and be purified by the blood of the lamb. Then fill your mind and spirit with the Word of God. Let God's Word fill you with compassion for others and a love that humbly serves God and man.

> *"When pride comes, then comes shame; But with the humble is wisdom."* Proverbs 11:2

> *"Humble yourself in the sight of the Lord, and He shall lift you up."* James 4:10

We are not to have pride. We are to be humble in our service to God and to others. What does being humble actually mean? To live humble means we are not proud or arrogant, but modest, content, courteous. We act with gentleness, we are polite, quiet, and respectful. It is apparent that we cannot be proud and also be humble at the same time. Having a humble spirit means we are kind and we think of others first. Being humble is the opposite of being proud which is assertive, boastful, and conceited. Though God's people are humble, it does not mean that they are easily fooled or controlled. No! We are bold as a lion and as gentle as a dove. We are in tune with the Spirit of God who tells us when it is time to fight a battle or when it's time to be still. With the Spirit of the Lord leading us, we have the correct amount of assertiveness for each situation we encounter.

> *"A man's pride will bring him low, But the humble in spirit will retain honor."*
> Proverbs 29:23

Do you find yourself getting impatient with others easily? Do you give your opinion on every topic? Do you get upset when people have a different opinion than you do? Do you become angry when you think you are being ignored? If you answered yes to any of these questions you may have a problem with pride and not even be aware of it.

If you think you have some characteristics of pride, repent and walk in humility. Read your Bible every day and God will help you to understand how to be humble. It is through the pages of His Word that we receive His quiet gentle spirit which transforms our thoughts and actions to be just like Him. He is humble and quiet in spirit and He never forces Himself on anyone, nor does He become angry when we don't follow His lead. He is a loving God who wants only to have a loving relationship with His children. He does not condemn us, but gently leads us as a father leads his children that they may learn and become wise from his teachings.

We can see that the pitfalls of pride are many, and unless we die to selfish pride we will be destroyed by it. Pride is sin and we know that the wages of sin is death. So purify yourself and live in humility as you honor God in your thoughts, words, and deeds. Boastfulness is empty and has no earthly or eternal value. It is by your actions and words that others will know you are a person of integrity, gentleness, and honor.

> *"Therefore humble yourselves under the mighty hand of God, that He may exalt you in due time, casting all your care upon Him, for He cares for you."* 1 Peter 5:6-7

Heavenly Father,

I come humbly before You today to repent of holding pride in my heart. I confess Jesus as Lord of my life and I choose to die to the selfish ways of pride. Lead me through Your Holy Spirit and through the teachings in Your Word, that I may learn to walk in humility as a child of God. Remind me to always put others before myself and to walk in integrity and honor unto You. Help me to remember to keep my eyes on You and keep me aware of the pitfalls of pride that I will never allow it to enter my heart again.

In Jesus' Name,
Amen

"For the day of the Lord of hosts shall come upon everything proud and lofty, Upon everything lifted up – And it shall be brought low." Isaiah 2:12

"...God resists the proud, But gives grace to the humble." James 4:6

DAY 13

Spending Time With God

> *"With my whole heart I have sought You; Oh, let me not wander from Your commandments! Your word have I hidden in my heart, that I might not sin against You. Blessed are You, O Lord! Teach me your statutes."* Psalms 119:10-12

When we seek the Lord with our whole heart, we will find Him. He does not hide from those who diligently seek Him. He desires for us to seek Him that He may reveal to us the deep treasures of His Word. We begin to see our life in a new light as we listen to God speak to us through His Word and as we communicate with Him in prayer. Our thoughts become peaceful and the confusion of our mind is dissolved. God is our Heavenly Father, and what loving father does not want to hear from his children? Daily He waits to hear from you personally. He wants you to bring to

Him all your cares, worries, and praises which will give Him permission to work in your life. The Lord is a gentleman and He will not intervene in any situation of your life without being invited. Stop blaming God for not giving you an outcome that you desired when you had failed to ask for Him to intervene.

> "*Yet you do not have because you do not ask. You ask and do not receive, because you ask amiss, that you may spend it on your pleasure.*" James 4:3

We must ask the Lord to help us and *speak in line with His Word* while standing on His promises. We need to allow Him to take care of our situation in His time. Never be in a hurry to get a quick answer. Once we have given our problem to God, it is not ours any longer. Our job is now to stand in faith, believing He will answer.

> "*Ask and it will be given to you; seek, and you will find; knock, and it will be open to you.*" Matthew 7:7

When we accepted Jesus as our Savior we became one with God. As we develop our understanding of His statutes, we grow in our spiritual wisdom of who He is and of who we are in Him. He will continue to teach us through His Spirit as we continue to seek His laws (Word).

> *"Seek the Lord while He may be found, call upon Him while He is near."* Isaiah 55:6

There is life in the Word of God. God is life, He gives life and His Word is alive. Our life is in God who gives generously to all who seek Him. He does not turn away those who are hungry to learn the good news proclaimed in His Word. His promises are for all who desire to know Him.

In the Bible we find *'God's Word'* defined in several ways. It is called His *statutes*, His *law*, His *ordinances*, His *judgments*, His *oracles*, His *testimony*, His *precepts*, and His *commandments*. God's Word has many ways in which it teaches, reaches and ministers to the multitude. It also has many ways of working in our lives through a variety of people.

God's Word saves, heals, rescues, restores, builds up, creates, lights the path, disciplines, reveals His treasures, shields from harm, balances, upholds, protects, holds together, instructs, gives understanding and wisdom, and leads all who seek Him with their whole heart. We are blessed beyond measure to be given the privilege to own and freely read the Word of God. America may have it's problems but we are still the greatest country on earth. We are blessed to have the choice to worship the Lord and to read the Word. We cannot take this blessing for granted. So, read the

Word of God, and thank Him every day that you are still allowed to do so.

Here are a few Scriptures that reveal how beneficial it is to spend time with God and His Word:

> "*You are my hiding place and shield; I hope in Your word*" Psalms 119:114. He hides us from harm and shields us.
>
> "*The unfolding of Thy words gives light...*" Psalms 119:130 NAS. He is our light.
>
> "*Unless your law had been my delight, I would have perished in my afflictions*" Psalms 119:92. He restores, shields and protects. He is our delight.
>
> "*I will never forget your precepts, for by them you have given me life*" Psalms 119:93. He instructs, leads and reveals as we meditate on His Word. He gives life.
>
> "*I will never leave you or forsake you*" Hebrews 13:5. He is continually with us.
>
> "*Teach me to do Your will, For you are my God; Your Spirit is good. Lead me in the land of uprightness*" Psalms

> 143:10. God teaches us to do good and live righteously.
>
> "*Cast your burden on the Lord, And He shall sustain you...*" Psalm 55:22. He takes our burdens, strengthens us and keeps us.

We must have faith in God's Word for it to be able to work in our life. Without faith in the Word, the Bible is just a book. Faith is an assurance and a confidence in what we believe is true. When we read the Word it becomes a seed in our spirit. That seed planted in our spirit will grow if we nourish it regularly by staying connected to that which gives it life. Jesus is life and His Word gives life to our spirit.

Spending time with God brings great rewards. It has value in this world and in our eternal home. It teaches us how to live and it gives us wisdom and understanding both here and in our eternal home. That which we learn and understand here on Earth from reading our Bible we won't need to be taught in our heavenly home. Yes, we will still be learning even in heaven. The more you learn of the oracles of God now, the less you will have to learn later. That's why our time spent with God is never wasted time. God's Word is eternal and it will never become obsolete. "*Heaven and earth will pass away, but My Word will by no means pass away.*" Matthew 24:35

God's Word is beautiful! It is my delight to find quiet time to spend in His Word. As I dig into the treasures of His statutes, His still calm voice speaks to my spirit with teachings, direction, and correction. I have learned more from my quiet time with God about His will and His ways than I have from all the ministers and teachers I have heard throughout my entire life. That's how important reading His Word is. God's Word is so rich in wisdom and knowledge, nothing can compare to it. I love basking in His presence with His Word opened before me. It speaks to my spirit and reveals to me things I could not have otherwise known.

> *"I will meditate on Your precepts, And contemplate Your ways, I will delight myself in Your statutes; I will not forget Your word."* Psalms 119:15-16

Do you find that you are spending very little time with God? Are you talking to God in prayer? Do you plan on reading His Word and praying but you never seem to have the time to follow through with your plans?

Let me encourage you today to make it a priority to spend quiet time with God. Share your day with Him and read His Word to find answers to your questions. If you don't understand the Bible, ask God to help you understand His Word and do not give up. You will soon find it easier to read. As previously mentioned, time is never wasted when we spend it with God. God will give you back the time you spend with Him. When you get the promises of God in your heart you will be storing up treasures in heaven. Today begin spending time with God!

> *"Do not lay up for yourselves treasures on earth, where moth and rust destroy and where thieves break in and steal; but lay up for yourselves treasures in heaven where neither moth nor rust destroys and where thieves do not break in and steal. For where your treasure is, there your heart will be also."* Matthew 6:19-21

> Heavenly Father,

> Thank you for Your Word which is an instruction manual for us to live by. As I read the Bible help me to understand and remember that which You are teaching me. I ask that You help me to live according to Your laws in everything I do. Forgive me for being lax in spending time with You. Remind me to set aside some time for quiet moments with You every day. I thank You for the many promises You give us in Your Word. I

know Your promises are true and we can rely on them.

In Jesus' Name,
Amen

"Good and upright is the Lord; therefore He teaches sinners in the way. The humble He guides in justice, and the humble He teaches His way. All the paths of the Lord are mercy and truth, to such as keep His covenant and His testimonies." Psalms 25:8-10

"He who despises the word will be destroyed, But he who fears the commandments will be rewarded." Proverbs 13:13

DAY 14

Prayer

> *"Watch and pray, lest you enter into temptations. The spirit indeed is willing but the flesh is weak."* Mark 14:38

What is prayer and what do we do when we pray? Prayer is visiting with God through conversation. It is a time we give God thanksgiving, and worship, and we make our petitions known to Him. It is not a time to complain about what is going wrong in our life. Yes we are to give our worries and cares to the Lord in prayer, but not in a complaining manner. With complete trust and faith in His ability to handle every situation in our life, we simply say, "Lord, I give You my burdens and I know You will take care of me." We pray knowing He will stand by the promises He has given to us in His Word.

> *"Cast all your cares on Him for He cares for you"* I Peter 5:7.

> *"Ask and it shall be given to you; seek, and you shall find; knock, and it will be opened to you."* Matthew 7:7

Praying to God is a privilege. People of the Old Testament weren't allowed this privilege. When they needed to talk to God, they had to go to the priest who would pray on their behalf. We are blessed to have a personal relationship with God through Jesus Christ, and that we have direct communication with Him.

According to Dictionary.com the word prayer is defined as, a spiritual communion with God, thanksgiving, adoration, or confession. It is petition, appeal, devotion, request, and worship to a deity. No where in this definition do we find that praying is complaining. We are to petition God for our needs and to make our request known. That is not complaining. We also pray to dedicate ourselves to Him and to worship Him.

There are several type of prayers. One type of prayers are the prayers that change things in our life. These prayers are for binding and loosening by coming into agreement with God's Word. Another type of prayer is to make our request known to God. There are prayers of adoration, declaration, thanksgiving, and worship. Whatever kind of prayer we are saying, we must always pray in line with God's will, purpose, and plan, according to His Word.

While we are spending time with God in prayer, we must not forget to praise Him for all the wonderful blessings we enjoy. We exalt the Lord as He takes our problems and replaces them with His peace. When we take our focus off of ourselves and turn our attention onto God, we will dwell in His peace.

> *"Peace I leave with you, My peace I give to you; not as the world gives do I give to you. Let not your heart be troubled, neither let it be afraid."* John 14:27

When we pray we must have faith that what we pray for will be done. Prayer without faith does not work. There is a song with a verse that says, prayer is the key to heaven and faith unlocks the door. Without faith our prayer is like a ship without an oar. And we know a ship without an oar goes nowhere. It is through believing that we have what we pray for and our prayers are answered. Without believing our prayer will not be beneficial to us.

> *"Therefore I say to you, whatever things you ask when you pray, believe that you receive them, and you will have them."* Mark 11:24

> *"And my God shall supply all your need according to His riches in glory by Christ Jesus."* Philippians 4:19

Prayer is not only talking to God, but it is also listening to Him. Praying is a two-way conversation. It is not just a single speaker with an audience of one. We need to be ready to listen to all He has to say to us. We should stay in a constant attitude of prayer, which means we should always be listening for the voice of the Lord and communicate with Him. And when we hear Him speak something into our heart, we are to obey Him. If we don't obey what He has told us to do, we are wasting our time praying to Him. Pray expecting to hear from Him.

Prayer was important to Jesus while He walked upon the earth. It was through prayer that He listened for His Father's instructions. In John 8:28 Jesus said, *"When you lift up the Son of Man, then you will know that I am He, and I do nothing of Myself; but as My Father taught Me, I speak these things."* Jesus didn't do anything without talking to His Father about it first. Why would we think we can figure out anything in our life on our own when even Jesus had to seek His Father's instructions? Are we smarter than Jesus that we don't need to gain instruction from God? And when we receive instruction we must obey it just as Jesus did when His Father talked to Him.

> *"Incline your ear, and come to Me. Hear, and your soul shall live."* Isaiah 55:3

Make sure your words and actions line up with your prayers. If we ask God for something then we speak against what we have asked for, we are hindering God in answering our prayers. If we ask according to the Word and we speak and act according to the Word, God will hear us and answer our petition. This is another reason it is important to know the Word of God. If we don't know the Word of God we ask amiss and our prayers are hindered. We get results when we pray God's Word back to Him. He stands by His Word and He will always do what He has said in His Word.

> *"So shall My word be that goes forth from My mouth; It shall not return to Me void, But it shall accomplish what I please, And it shall prosper in the thing for which I sent it."* Isaiah 55:11

There are many reasons why we should pray. Visiting with God is important. It is a time of worship and praise. It is a time to make our petitions known to God, and in prayer we can bind or loose in agreement with the Word. We give our cares to God in prayer and in turn He gives us peace and joy. Turning our cares over to the Lord lifts us up and places our focus back onto Him, instead of on our problems. The plan's God has for us are far greater than anything we could imagine for ourselves. Seek Him through the pages of His Word. Talk with Him in prayer and listen to His direction.

> *"Assuredly, I say to you, whatever you bind on earth will be bound in heaven,*

and whatever you loose on earth will be loosed in heaven." Matthew 18:18

"In my distress I prayed to the Lord, and the Lord answered me and set me free." Psalm 118:5

Heavenly Father,

I thank You for the privilege of being able to come to You in prayer. As one who loves Your Word and strives to live according to it, I know You hear my prayers. You are always ready and excited to hear from Your children. Thank You for the prayer of petition where I can lay down my troubles at Your feet and leave them there and You replacing them with Your peace. I also thank You for the prayers of thanksgiving that I may express my love and trust in You. Lead me and guide me into a deeper prayer life that I may become well acquainted with basking in Your presence and hearing Your voice throughout each day. You are an awesome God and nothing compares to You! What an honor to call upon You and know by faith that You will answer.

In Jesus' Name
Amen

"For I know the thoughts that I think towards you, says the Lord, thoughts of peace and not of evil, to give you a future and a hope. Then you will call upon Me and go and pray to Me, and I will listen to you. And you will seek Me and find Me, when you search for Me with all your heart." Jeremiah 29:11-13

"Now this is the confidence that we have in Him, that if we ask anything according to His will, He hears us. And if we know that He hears us, whatever we ask, we know that we have the petitions that we have asked of Him." 1 John 5:14

DAY 15

Read God's Word

> "Heaven *and earth shall pass away, but My words will by no means pass away."*
> Mark 13:31

We need to stay in the Word of God to have our mind renewed. We come to God by confessing our sins and receiving Jesus as our Savior. It is through His blood that our sins are washed away, but we still have the old sinful way of thinking. Our mind is renewed by reading the Word of God, but not by reading God's Word just once. Our mind is renewed as we read the Bible daily. Without the Word in our mind, we will think, talk, and act like the world. The world speaks negative and talks of death, but God's Word speaks positive and talks of life. Negative thinking is not in agreement with the Word. The negative thoughts that ruled your mind will leave you as you fill your mind with scriptures. Studying the Bible will reveal God's will and ways to you, and it gives you insight to His purpose and plans.

> *"And do not be conformed to this world, but be transformed by the renewing of your mind, that you may prove what is that good and acceptable will of God."*
> Romans 12:2

Read the Word and speak the scriptures out loud. Just as we eat food and it becomes a part of us to give our physical body strength and nourishment, we also absorb the spoken Word of God as we read it out loud because it is our spiritual food. We will not grow strong spiritually without reading God's Word. When our thinking is trained on the Word of God, we will begin to act upon that which we have learned.

It is also very important to attend a faith based church that is preaching the true anointed Word of God. There are many churches to choose from, so we need to ask God in prayer to reveal to us the church He wants us to attend. There is a church God will assign for you to attend where you will learn, grow, and minister. It is up to each of us to find out where our place is and attend that fellowship faithfully. The right church with the right pastor will make all the difference in your spiritual growth. It must be where the Word of God is believed, and preached from cover to cover. If you have found a church but you think that the full truth of the Word is not being taught or encouraged, you need to move on and find the right church. Let God make the decision for you. Only where He wants you to attend is where you will spiritually mature and be of the greatest use to God and to your fellow believers.

> *"And you shall know the truth, and the truth shall make you free."* John 8:32

Be faithful in reading the Word. Reading God's Word needs to be a daily priority due to the fact that our mind is renewed through a day by day process of hearing the Word. We learn a little at a time, precept upon precept (Isaiah 28:10). Daily, add more knowledge of the Word to your thinking. Your thinking affects how you believe and your believing affects how you act. When you are filled up with your daily portion of the Word, you will begin to act according to the Word that is in you. The Word planted in your mind produces right thinking and you begin speaking in agreement with God. Whatever is in you will come out of you. Whether we're a believer or a non-believer, our words and actions tell what is in our heart. *"A good man out of the good treasure of his heart brings forth good; and an evil man out of the evil treasure of his heart brings forth evil. For out of the abundance of the heart his mouth speaks,"* Luke 6:45.

We cannot hide the kind of person we are when we open our mouth the truth is revealed.

> *"For as many as are lead by the Spirit of God, these are the sons of God."* Romans 8:14

Having great knowledge in the Word of God helps us in all areas of our life. It lifts us up when we are down. It directs us when a decision needs to be made. It protect us from the enemy of our soul. It encourages us, strengthens us, builds our faith, gives us wisdom, and understanding in things we otherwise would not know. The Word lights our path even in unfamiliar territory. The benefits of knowing the Word of God are too numerous to count. But you will not know the Word of God if you don't read it.

> *"So then faith comes by hearing, and hearing by the word of God."* Romans 10:17

> *"Study to shew thyself approved unto God, a workman that need not be ashamed, rightly dividing the word of truth."* 2 Timothy 2:15 KJV

The Word of God is a letter written to followers of God. If you are a follower of God, then His book is written to you. You are to read it, study it, know it, live by it, and teach it. God's book is a love letter to us. It is an instruction manual informing us how to live righteously. It is a light to direct us and keep us on the right path. It is a history book that tells stories of those who were sinners long ago. And it shares stories of courageous men who walked close with God through trials, and in doing so were triumphant in victory over the enemy. We are to learn from their stories that we may also walk close to God and not make the mistakes others have made in the past. It is an honor and a privilege to have the Word of God to study that we may learn how to live a godly life and minister to others. Without God's Word, how could we ever know about our wonderful Heavenly Father and His Son Jesus? When we know God's Word, we know God. Get to know God at a deeper level by studying the Bible daily. You will see a change for the better in your thinking and in your life.

> *"For whatever things were written before were written for our learning, that we through the patience and comfort of the Scriptures might have hope."* Romans 15:4

> *"Therefore, having these promises, beloved, let us cleanse ourselves from all filthiness of flesh and spirit, perfecting holiness in the fear of God."* 1 Corinthians 7:1

Heavenly Father,

Thank You for Your Word. It is a blessing to have the freedom to be able to study the Bible. Remind me each day to sit quietly and meditate on the Scriptures that I may receive understanding of Your ways. As my mind is renewed with Your Word, help me to be bold and speak to others about what the Scriptures have taught me. Thank You for all You have done in giving us Your Word.

In Jesus' Name
Amen

"*You are my hiding place and my shield; I hope in Your word.*" Psalm 119:114

"*Your word is a lamp to my feet and a light to my path.*" Psalm 119:105

DAY 16

Consecrate Do Not Deviate

> *"Therefore, do not throw away your confidence, which has a great reward. For you have need of endurance, so that when you have done the will of God, you may receive what was promised....But we are not of those who shrink back to destruction, but of those who have faith to the preserving of the soul."* Hebrews 10:35, 36, 39 NAS

We who are followers of Jesus cannot lose our confidence in the value of our commitment to the Lord. Our eternal reward is based upon our commitment to Christ through our faith. If we are truly living in faith we will reap the goodness of what we sow as our reward. We must endure through trials with determination to be set apart and be consecrated unto God. True followers of Jesus must never allow trials or persecution to cause them to deviate from their dedication of living according to the call of God. We are privileged to live in His righteousness with a life dedicated unto His service.

> *"For He delivered us from the domain of darkness, and transferred us to the kingdom of His beloved Son, in whom we have redemption, the forgiveness of sins."* Colossians 1:13-14 NAS

> *"So that you may walk in the manner of the God who calls you into His own kingdom and glory."* 1 Thessalonians 2:12 NAS

Being useful for the kingdom requires a commitment to living according to God's will and plan for your life. How do you know what God's plan is for your life? You can know His plan by reading His Word and by spending time with Him in prayer. We know His will when we have a close relationship with Him as our Father and as the Lord of our life. When we serve Him as Lord our greatest desire will be to allow Him to lead us. Following the leading of the Holy Spirit will keep us on the straight path and will not allow any deviation. If we find ourselves on a path that is not in line with the Word of God, it is we who have turned ourselves from the path, it was not Jesus who lead us there. It is vitally important to continually keep our eyes on Jesus as we go through each day. Any time we take our eyes off of our Lord and put them on ourselves it can open a door to the enemy of our soul, whose main purpose is to kill, steal, and destroy.

Be committed to serve God in all areas of your life. With a complete consecrated heart we reap the full benefits as a child of God. Jesus did not deviate from His purpose in fulfilling the Father's plan for His life. Jesus had set Himself apart for that one purpose. And just like Jesus, we are not to deviate from our dedication of living and ministering for God. We do this by setting ourselves apart, living consecrated to His sacred purpose and being wholly devoted to the Word of God. When God's Word is inscribed upon our heart, our desire will only be that which our Father desires. But without His Word in us we can easily be lead astray and fall from grace.

> *"Cease listening to instructions, my son,*
> *And you will stray from the words of knowledge."* Proverbs 19:27

We see on Dictionary.com, the word 'consecrate' means to dedicate, devote, sanctify, and set apart. And the word 'deviate' means to fall from grace, sin, bend the rules, turn aside, go astray, and wander. So when we do not consecrate ourselves to the service of God we fail to be set apart for Him. That allows us to deviate from living in faith, which eventually results in our turning aside and wandering from the path of the Lord. Believers are to renew their mind every day with the fresh Word of God. Reading the Word will keep us on track, give us wisdom, guide our decisions, and encourage us when we go through trials. And having the Word renewed in us every day will allow us to be ready in season and out of season to minister to those in need. Without the Word in us, how can we give to others what we do not have?

Be devoted to reading the Word of God and communicating with him in prayer. Make it a daily habit to bask in His presence and listen to His voice. To be a consecrated Christian, we must make seeking God a priority every day. Never give the devil a chance to gain a foothold and cause you to deviate from the path God has set you on. We are to keep our eyes on Jesus and not on those things around us, nor replay past regrets over and over in our mind. The replaying of the negative past thoughts will open a door that you don't want opened. Seal up all areas of your life, past, present, and future with the living Word of God. The enemy can't kill, steal, or destroy what he is not allowed access to.

> *"...forgetting those things which are behind and reaching forward to those things which are ahead. I press toward the goal for the prize of the upward call of God in Christ Jesus."* Philippians 3:13b-14

Do you desire to draw closer to God? Are you lax in your commitment to serving God? Is Jesus Lord of your life, or are you drawn away from serving Him with your whole heart? Have you deviated from the path of living a life of righteousness?

Today, consecrate yourself to be holy and set apart for God. Practice following His leading and be determined to never deviate from the path of righteousness.

> *"But as He who called you is holy, you also be holy in your conduct, because it is written, "Be holy, for I am holy"* 1 Peter 1:15-26.
>
> Heavenly Father,
>
> Thank You for Your Son Jesus who gave us the example of how to live holy. I will be diligent to spend time in Your presence daily as I consecrate myself to serving You as my Lord and Savior. Keep me on the path of righteousness that the enemy of my soul will not be given access to me. And remind me to not open any doors to the enemy by the words I speak or the things I do. I am determined to be set apart to serve You and I will not deviate from Your Word.

Thank You for sanctifying me through the blood of Jesus.

In Jesus' Name
Amen

"And for their sakes I sanctify Myself; that they also may be sanctified by the truth." John 17:19

"...Sanctify yourselves, for tomorrow the Lord will do wonders among you." Joshua 3:5

"Blow the trumpet in Zion, Consecrate a fast, Call a sacred assembly;" Joel 2:15

DAY 17

Stand Strong In the Lord

> "*...Be strong in the Lord and the power of His might.*" *Ephesians 6:10*

Death and life are in the power of the tongue (Proverbs 18:21). Those who have their life rooted in Christ will speak forth life. We command our body, mind, and spirit to come in line with the Word of God. And the Word of God says, "*He was wounded for our transgressions, He was bruised for our iniquities; the chastisement for our peace was upon Him, and by His stripes we are healed*" (Isaiah 53:5). This verse says ARE healed which is NOW! We are ALREADY healed! Our healing was completed on the cross of Calvary when Jesus paid the ransom for our sins and sicknesses. When the enemy tries to put illness on you, tell him he has no authority to do so. As a born again child of God you have all the promises in the Bible as your very own, and Satan has no right to destroy you by any means. The only right he has to bring you harm is the rights you give him by agreeing with him instead of agreeing with the Word.

The Word of God also says, "*No weapon formed against us shall prosper*" (Isaiah 54:17), which means no matter what the enemy throws at us it will not prevail to bring us down. However, it is up to us to stand strong on all the promises of God. We cannot just know the promises in the Word, but we have to act upon them and exercise our authority over the enemy. Command the devil to leave and to take his hands off of you and your household. *Therefore, submit to God. Resist the devil and he will flee from you*" (James 4:7). We are to submit to God, not to the devil. When we submit to the devil he has our permission to bring havoc into our lives. We need to"*Draw near to God and He will draw near to you*" (James 4:8). And we need to, "*Humble yourself in the sight of the Lord, and He will lift you up*" (James 4:10). As we come humbly before the throne of grace, God will lift us up above our circumstances and set us on higher ground out of the reach of the enemy.

> "*For in the time of trouble He will hide me in His pavilion; In the secret place of His tabernacle he shall hide me; He shall set me high upon a rock*" Psalm 27:5.

We who have salvation and love the Lord with all our heart need not be afraid of anything the devil attempts to do to us. Salvation means safety, preservation, healing, prosperity, soundness of mind, and deliverance. We have all of this as part of our salvation through the blood of Jesus.

> *"For God hasn't given us a spirit of fear, but of power and of love and of a sound mind."* 2 Timothy 2:7

Be bold and stand on your rightful authority as a child of God. When God is on the throne of your heart, the devil is weak against you. Visualize Satan in a paper bag fighting with all his might to break through to get to you, but the bag is too strong for him. That's how it is for all of us who are covered under the mighty hand of God. Though the devil rages against us, he is not able to bring us harm when we stay strong in the Lord. We are protected as long as we keep our focus on the Lord and abide in the Word of God which is our strength. The enemy will fight against all that we stand for, but Jesus has already won the battle. The victory belongs to us, to all those who believe and follow close to Jesus. Watch and see the hand of God move on your behalf. Receive your healing and deliverance, the victory is yours! Take it!

> *"Eye has not seen, nor ear heard, Nor have entered into the heart of man the*

> *things which God has prepared for those who love Him."* 1 Corinthians 2:9

Walk in faith and receive the provisions God has for you. See with your spiritual eyes what God has waiting for you and finish your race in victory. Never give up! Stay the course! Keep your eyes on God! Live boldly for Jesus in the ministry He has called you to do and complete your assignment. Stand strong in the Lord!

> *"Look unto Jesus the author and finisher of our faith, who for the joy that was set before Him endured the cross, despising the shame, and has sat down at the right hand of the throne of God."* Hebrews 12:2

> *"Have I not commanded you? Be strong and of good courage; do not be afraid, nor be dismayed, for the Lord your God is with you wherever you go."* Joshua 1:9

Throughout the Bible we are encouraged to stay in faith and not doubt. God is on our side. He is always with us and waits to be asked to intervene. God does not help without being asked. And if we ask for His help, we must yield to His plan and His ways. In other words, we are to give our situation to God and get out of His way so He can resolve our problem. You can rest assured He has your back. God always makes a way when we leave our burdens with Him. He will set everything right that we give to Him if we stand in faith, and speak faith over the situation. See with your spiritual eyes the troubles resolved the way God sees them.

> *"For it is He who delivers you from the snare of the trapper. And from the deadly pestilence He will cover you with His pinions and under His wings you may seek refuge. His truth shall be your shield and buckler."* Psalm 91:3-4

Today get into the Word and seek out the promises which God has given you. When you know the promises, then you will know the scriptures to stand on for each situation you face. When the enemy shoots fiery arrows at you remember, you have the shield of God's Word to protect you. So stand strong in the Lord and take your authority as a child of the Most High God.

> *"Stand therefore, having girded your waist with truth, having put on the breastplate of righteousness, and having shod your feet with the preparation of the gospel of peace; above all, taking the shield of faith with which you will be able to quench all the fiery darts of the wicked one. And take the helmet of salvation, and the sword of the Spirit, which is the Word of God."* Ephesians 6:14-17

Heavenly Father,

Thank You for the many promises You have given us to stand on through the storms of life. I know as I faithfully seek Your Word, You will help me stand up against the enemy with boldness as I take the authority You have given me. Help me to keep my eyes on You and not on the circumstances that surround me. Jesus has already given me the victory over all the traps of the devil. Thank You for being my comfort and my help in time of need and always.

In Jesus' Name
Amen

"Therefore take up the whole armor of God, that you may be able to withstand in the evil day, and having done all, to stand." Ephesians 6:13

"When my heart is overwhelmed, lead me to that rock that is higher than I." Psalm 61:2b

"For the law of the Spirit of life in Christ Jesus has made me free from the law of sin and death." Romans 8:2

DAY 18

A Rock On The Path

> *"For I am not ashamed of the gospel of Christ, for it is the power of God to salvation for everyone who believes..."*
> *Romans 1:16 a*

As I continue to serve the Lord and study His Word I draw closer to Him. The Lord opens doors to new areas of service in ministry. After many years of seeking Him and His plan for my life, I believe I am finally on the right path where I can produce much fruit for God's kingdom. I am pleased to be able to minister to a wider range of people than I had in the past. Everything seemed to be coming together just as God had planned, and I had hoped. Until suddenly one day there was a very large rock in my path. This is the vision I was given about that rock:

Though this was the path I prayed to be on, a large rock was blocking my path. This was the path which I believed God had placed me on. The path gently ascended up the mountain which represented a higher level of service to God. At the top of the mountain was complete victory where we will hear the voice of the Lord say, "*Well done, My good and faithful servant.*"

A knowing in my spirit said I had to stay on the path to reach the top of the mountain, so I prayed for the rock to move, but it didn't. I tried to move the rock by my strength, but I couldn't. I thought I'd climb over it, but it was to large. I paced and thought and prayed about the rock, but it didn't move. I cried to God and pleaded for Him to move the rock for me, but He didn't move it. So I decided to dig under the rock, but the ground was too hard. I tried to go around the rock, but it was so large that I found myself way off the path. I knew I needed to complete my journey on the right path so I returned to where I had started.

I spoke to the rock commanding it to be gone, to move, and to vanish. But it did not leave, move or vanish. I stood there refusing to waver. I rebuked it and took authority over it, but it did not move. I had done all I knew to do and yet it continued to block my path.

Unsure why God did not move the rock for me, I walked away in frustration. I began busying myself in other areas of service and tried to keep my mind off of that stubborn rock. I still thought about it and prayed about it but I decided to not allow it to consume my time. In my busyness, as I continued to minister, I discovered the Lord was able to use me to minister in ways I hadn't thought of before and I was excited to be useful in these new areas.

As the days and the weeks passed the rock that had blocked my path was hardly even a thought to me. Then one day the room began to shake. The books tumbled off the shelves in my office and everything swayed. I looked out of the window and saw trees wave to and fro as the earth quaked beneath them. When the rumbling stopped and everything became still, I looked at the mountain in the distance. I was amazed to see the rock that frustrated me so was now at the bottom of the mountain and had broken into several small pieces. In my surprise I said, "Lord, the rock is gone. Now I can continue on the path of ministry you had placed me on. Why didn't that rock move for me before?"

I heard the Lord answer in my spirit saying, *"You had more things to learn before you were ready to continue in that ministry. In the new areas you are now working I was able to teach you what you were lacking. Now you are wiser and stronger and ready to continue on the path. Keep your mind open to possibilities in ministry. Don't be narrow minded. I can only use my people in areas of ministry that they are open to, but I have many areas in which I need to use them.*

When you stop to rest and pray I can show you My plan. When you wait on Me, new doors will open. Even though I may set a goal before you, you are to continually check with Me to reaffirm your next step. When a rock appears on your path sometimes the enemy is trying to block your work and at other times it is I telling you to wait. During these times of waiting I may teach you something new before you continue on the path, or I may be telling you to wait because I know there is danger on the path ahead of you. You will know the difference between the enemy attempting to stop you or Me telling you to wait. If it's the enemy when you rebuke the rock and ask Me to move it, it will move as you stand in faith and take your authority over the enemy. But if it is I who is blocking your path no amount of pleading will move the rock because I am telling you to wait. When you have learned what you needed to learn and the path is free from harm, the rock will move. Pray continually so that you stay on the right path. Be not deceived!"

Through His message God had disclosed a new revelation to me. He taught me that when we are ministering effectively but suddenly we hit a brick wall, our progress will depend on our ability to wait and pray. Some people refuse to wait. They forge ahead determined to keep moving forward. They go around the rock which takes them off the path God had set them on and the consequences of their actions can mean an end to their ministry. It is for our benefit and spiritual growth to wait patiently when God says to wait.

> "*...Offer to God an acceptable service with reverence and awe.*" Hebrew 12:28c NAS

God also taught me that not every barrier we come to on our journey is from Satan. Sometimes the rock blocking our path is God telling us to stop, wait, and pray. If we are wise we will heed His warning. This is not an excuse to become lazy in our service to God. When God says to wait and pray we are to be obedient and do it. We must learn to wait patiently as we seek the Lord's will through prayer, but as we wait and pray we need to keep ourselves actively working in any area God brings us to. Just because God says to wait and pray it doesn't mean that we should walk away from our the service unto Him. A rock in our path should signal a time to refresh, restore, and renew our spiritual service unto Him. It is a time to rest, but also a time to grow and gain strength for what lies ahead. And it is a time to listen and learn. Be open to hear what He has to say to you. Yield to His direction to stay on the right path.

With a fresh awareness of God's plan we are able to continue on the path of ministry He has assigned to us. Always remember to stay close to the Lord as He leads you on your journey in sharing the good news of His redemption and love.

> *"Therefore, my beloved brethren, be steadfast, immovable, always abounding in the work of the Lord, knowing that your labor is not in vain in the Lord."* 1 Corinthians 15:58

> *"Wait on the Lord; Be of good courage, And he shall strengthen your heart; Wait, I say, on the Lord!"* Psalm 27:14

Heavenly Father,

Thank You for protecting me as I work in Your service. I will be cautious to be more aware of Your voice telling me to stop, wait, and pray. I will wait patiently as I seek Your will and Your plan on this journey You have placed me on. I know You are always with me and You have created me for this purpose of serving You through ministry unto others. Help me to fulfill my calling for Your glory.

In Jesus' Name
Amen

"Watch yourselves, that you might not lose what we have accomplished, but

that you may receive a full reward." 2 John 8 NAS

"Now the God of peace, who brought up from the dead the great Shepherd of the sheep through the blood of the eternal covenant, even Jesus our Lord, equip you in every good thing to do His will, working in us that which is pleasing in His sight, through Jesus Christ, to whom the glory forever and ever. Amen. Hebrews 13:20-21 NAS

DAY 19

The Truth and Nothing But The Truth

> *"If anyone teaches otherwise and does not consent to wholesome words, even the words of our Lord Jesus Christ, and to the doctrine which accords to godliness, he is proud, knowing nothing, but is obsessed with dispute and arguments over words, from which come envy, strife, reviling, evil suspicions, useless wranglings of men of corrupt minds and destitute of the truth, who suppose that godliness is a means of gain. From such withdraw yourself."* 1 Timothy 6:3-5

Be careful to only listen to those who preach the true Jesus who is the deity of the Trinity. According to 2 Corinthians 11:4, men can receive another spirit other than the Spirit of God and they can receive another gospel other than the gospel of Jesus Christ. These other spirits and gospels sound like, and appear to be, the real truth, but they are counterfeit who seek out the loyalty of man. Like Satan who transforms himself into an angel of light, these false teachers appear to be ministers of righteousness, yet they deny the righteousness of Jesus and preach that Jesus was only a good man.

> *"For such are false apostles, deceitful workers, transforming themselves into apostles of Christ. And no wonder! For Satan himself transforms himself into an angel of light."* 2 Corinthians 11:13-14

Many people will believe and follow these counterfeit preachers. But just because people believe in something does not make what they are preaching to be true. Anything that does not match up with the Word of God is false teaching. Too often people twist the scriptures to say what they want them to say. We cannot accept that kind of interpretation as truth. We read in Revelation 22:18-19, "*...If anyone adds to these things, God will add to him the plagues that are written in this book; and if anyone takes away from the words of the book of this prophecy, God shall take away his part from the Book of Life, from the holy city, and from the things which are written in this book."* God gives this warning because He takes it very seriously if we add to or take away anything He has written in His Word. Taking away from the scriptures is removing words to change the meaning to make it say what you want it to say and mean something different than God meant. And adding to the Word is the act of including words not originally said by the Spirit of God to the prophets. Either adding words to the scriptures or taking words away from it is twisting the scriptures from their intended meaning to benefit your own interpretation.

"For we can do nothing against the truth, but for the truth" 2 Corinthians 13:8.

This verse tells us to stand on the truth. The truth of God is always truth and does not change. In 1 John 2:21 we are told that "*no lie is of the truth.*" So, if what someone is preaching or teaching does not say that Jesus is deity and part of the Trinity, then their teaching in error. Don't listen to them. They will confuse your thoughts and put doubt in your mind. These false teachers have taken some scriptures and twisted them to say something other than what the true Word actually says in order to sway you for their own gain. We are to be "*sanctified in the truth of the Word*" (John 17:17), then we will *"know the truth and the truth shall set us free*" (John 8:32).

When we know the truth in our spirit, then the self-made preachers who preach something other than truth will not be able to entice us with fancy words and their great oracle abilities. When we have our feet planted firmly on the solid foundation of the Word, we will not be swayed to follow false teachings. We are those who abide in the vine, which is Jesus the Word, and He abides in us.

> *"I am the true vine, and My Father is the vine dresser. Every branch in Me that does not bear fruit He takes away; and every branch that bears fruit He prunes, that it may bear more fruit. You are already clean because of the word which I have spoken to you. Abide in Me, and I in you. As the branch cannot bear fruit of itself, unless you abide in Me."* John 15:1-4

We are to follow after Christ only! Never follow man on the grounds of what he has to say or for what he may offer you. Follow the leading of the Holy Spirit and He will lead you to those who are of sound teachings and are preaching the truth. The Holy Spirit will never change something that God has said in His Word. The Holy Spirit agrees with God's Word always and He will never lead you astray. This is another reason why we need to know what is in the Word of God. It is so we will not be lead astray by enticing words of false religions and preachers. We know the truth when the truth is in us. We must know God's Word so clearly that when false words are served up we know not to partake of them. God wants us to profess the truth and nothing but the truth in all we say and do. We are to confess the truth of His Word as a righteous child of God living the testimony of our salvation. Without His truth dwelling in us we have no righteousness. All of our righteousness is in Him and from Him. He is truth and there is no deceit within Him.

> *"You who love the Lord, hate evil! He preserves the souls of His saints; He delivers them out of the hands of the wicked."* Psalms 97:10

Sharpen your spiritual radar by reading the Word of God daily. It will keep you aware of those who would desire to draw you away into false teachings. With the Word of truth in our heart and minds we will shut down every deceitful word that comes against the truth.

If you are weak in this area, increase your time with the Lord through reading His Word and talking to Him through prayer. Time spent with God helps us to stay aware of the lies of the enemy and enables us to nullify every lying tongue which sets itself against the Word of God.

> *"...speak the things which are proper for sound doctrine..."* Titus 2:1

Heavenly Father,

Thank You for the truth of Your Word and for revealing to me those who would try to draw me away from Your truth. Help me to stay alert by keeping Your Word ever before me that my faith in You will not be shaken by false teachings. I thank You that Your Word is forever true. It is reassuring to know that You do not change and that I can always trust in You.

In Jesus' Name,
Amen

"But there were also false prophets among the people, even as there will be false teachers among you, who will secretly bring in destructive heresies, even denying the Lord who bought them, and bring on themselves swift destruction." 2 Peter 2:1

"And you shall know the truth, and the truth shall make you free." John 8:32

DAY 20

No Compromise

> *"Therefore, to him who knows to do good and does not do it, to him it is sin."* James 4:17

One of the greatest tactics of the devil is to get a believer to compromise what they believe. Just as he sheepishly slithered in the garden and placed doubt in the minds of Adam and Eve, Satan still uses that same sneaky plan today, asking, "Is that really what God said?"

According to Dictionary.com doubt means to question, to hesitate, uncertainty, distrust, faithlessness, and fear. When we allow the enemy to cause us to question anything God has said, we open our mind to doubt. When doubt takes root it produces compromise. People may think they are solid and never compromise their beliefs or turn from anything God has said; but we need to ask ourselves if we are standing strong on everything God says, or are we just standing strong on certain commands of God. When we decide there are some of God's commands to follow and other ones we can ignore, then we are compromising.

> *"Blessed are those who keep His testimonies, who seek Him with the whole heart! They also do no iniquity; They walk in His ways."* Psalms 119:2-3

When asked to do something that you know is wrong, do you think about possibly doing it? And do you go ahead and do it, thinking no one will know? That is compromising. When you take your groceries to your car in a cart, do you take the time to return the cart to the cart corral when you are finished with it? If not, that is compromising your integrity. Do you allow your fleshly desires to talk you out of attending church? That is also compromising with the flesh.

When we know what the right thing is to do in the eyes of God, and we have the opportunity to do what is right and the capability to do so, but we don't do it, it is sin (James 4:17).

> *"For if you live according to the flesh you will die; but if by the Spirit you put to death the deeds of the body, you will live. For as many as are led by the Spirit of God, these are sons of God."* Romans 8:13-14

Fear also brings compromise. Allowing fear to rule your life will compromise your faith. We need to remember that doubt and fear comes from the Satan. When we have fear of being ridiculed for doing something for God, we compromise our faith. By allowing fear to stop us from doing what we know we should do we compromise our christian witness. Boldly step out in faith and refuse to allow fear to take root in your mind. Refuse to compromise God's perfect plan for you.

Compromise means to settle for something different or to make concessions or to negotiate. As a follower of Jesus we cannot allow the devil to negotiate with us. We need to shut him down immediately when he comes to us bringing doubt or fear or the idea that we need to compromise. The Bible tells us, "*Therefore submit to God. Resist the devil and he will flee from you. Draw near to God and he will draw near to you. Cleanse your hands, you sinners and purify your hearts, you double-minded.*" James 4:7-8

Have you ever been in a situation where you were asked to speak up for the Lord, or sing His glory in front of a group of people and fear caused you to tremble so much that you decided not to do it? That is compromise. Fear is another favorite way used by the Satan to tempt believers to compromise. When the devil brings fear to us, we need to keep our mind on God and remember God's purpose for our sharing the good news of the gospel. We know God is working through us and we must stand strong and move forward with God. The Lord commands us to be strong and courageous (Joshua 1:9). With faith in God to bring about the outcome he desires, we can step out into new territory to minister for the Lord. Our comfort zone doesn't always have to be in place when we know we are walking step by step with the Lord. We have nothing to fear. God is on our side and He will bring us through every obstacle the enemy throws at us. Don't allow fear to cause you to compromise what God has called you to do.

> *"For God hasn't given us the spirit of fear, but of power and of love and of a sound mind."* 2 Timothy 1:7

Our love for God and His Word should keep us from shying away from sharing Christ with others. We are to be bold in our spirit and tell all who will listen. We cannot change the message of the gospel because of who we are talking to. Stick to the Word of God with all honesty and integrity so the truth of God will be proclaimed. When we are nervous in speaking up about our relationship with Jesus we can ask God to lead us by His Holy Spirit. He will answer our prayer and give us boldness. You will be amazed at the Bible scriptures you actually know to say at the right time. That is the Holy Spirit at work in you. You are the messenger, but it is God who speaks through your spirit.

> *"...Whoever desires to come after Me, let him deny himself, and take up the cross, and follow Me."* Mark 8:34b

A life that does not compromise the Word of God to please people is a life that God can use. When we allow intimidation from man to cause us to water down the truth of God's Word we change His message. We are to say what God tells us to say and leave the results to God. Remembering always to deliver God's Truth with the same love and compassion that drew us to the cross of salvation. If our motives are right in sharing the gospel and we share the uncompromising Word with love, then God's purpose will be accomplished. Always be sensitive to the leading of the Holy Spirit. In doing so you will have the right words to say every time to those who question the truth in you. God has given each and everyone of us a ministry to teach and reach the lost. Don't say, "I'm not a minister." We are all ministers to do the work of Jesus according to Matthew 28:19-20. If you have accepted the Lord as your Savior, then you are qualified to minister the gospel to the lost. Don't compromise the wisdom God has given you to minister to others.

> *"Go therefore and make disciples of all the nations, baptizing them in the*

> *name of the Father and the Son and the Holy Spirit, teaching them to observe all things that I have commanded you; and lo, I am with you always, even to the end of the age."* Matthew 28:19-20

These are the marching orders from our Lord. That makes every one of us ministers of the gospel of Christ. We are drafted into the Lord's army to fulfill His commands. Our fighting gear is the sword of the Spirit, which is the Word of God, and the shield of faith. Our assignment is to follow the leading of the Holy Spirit and to share the gospel with a dying world without compromising.

When a soldier compromises his assignment he lets down his shield and becomes an easy target for the enemy. Standing your ground with all of your armor on will defeat the enemy. And do not become weary in doing that which the Lord has sent you to do. Stay in God's Word to maintain your strength and understanding of the plan, purpose, and will of God in every area. Never jeopardize your standing as a faithful minister of His Word by compromising with the enemy. Be proactive with the Word of God and NEVER compromise His orders for anyone or for anything. God will protect you as you continue working in the calling He has placed on you.

Follow the Holy Spirit as He directs you in how and when to share, and do not deviate from what He says to do. It doesn't matter how strange it may sound to you, do it anyway that the uncompromising spoken Word will have it's way in their heart.

> *"But it is good for me to draw near to God; I have put my trust in the Lord God, that I may declare all Your works."* Psalm 73:28

Heavenly Father,

I give You praise and honor for the truth of Your Word which never compromises. I know all You have promised will come to pass in my life if I stay away from doubt and fear and stand strong on Your Word. Help me to fulfill the commands You have spoken to me that I may never allow compromising Your Word to have any part in my life. Out of the abundance of my heart I speak forth the good treasures from Your Word and the message of the cross. Thank You for spiritually maturing me that I may be used to reach the lost without compromising Your purpose.

In Jesus' Name
Amen

"He who believes in Me, as the scripture has said, 'out of his heart will flow rivers of living water'." John 7:38

"Stand therefore, having girded your waist with truth, having put on the breastplate of righteousness, and having shod your feet with the preparations of the gospel of peace; above all, take the shield of faith with which you will be able to quench all the fiery darts of the wicked one. And take the helmet of salvation, and the sword of the Spirit, which is the Word of God;..." Ephesians 6:14-17

DAY 21

Wake Up Before You Die

> *"A little sleep, a little slumber, A little folding of the hands to rest; So shall your poverty come like a prowler, And your need like an armed man."* Proverbs 24:33-34

Our need will overtake us if we are sleeping and not tending to physical requirements and spiritual matters. People are so mistaken when they put off making a commitment to God. They assume there will be time later to live for God, but right now they want to do their own thing. This is a very dangerous lifestyle. Poverty of things will come upon us when we are lazy, but worse than that is the poverty we find in our soul when we are alienated from God. No one is promised tomorrow. We are taking chances with our eternal destination when we put off having a personal relationship with God. Our last breath may happen so quickly that we won't have time to repent of our sins and make things right with God.

We are to be about our Father's business, which means live for Him today and accomplish what He created us for. We live in great blessings when we learn how to hear God as He speaks to us through the pages of His Word and through the Holy Spirit. It is time to get busy and remove laziness from our lives. Get rid of sin and guilt while there is still time. Don't be a person who is held captive through fleshly pleasures in leisure and self indulgence. A lazy person is addicted to sleep and has very little interest in work, but a wise person works hard to feed his family and seek the will of God. The Bible tells us our reward will be great for being committed in all that God created us for.

Trust God to supply for your every need as you grow in wisdom through the pages of His Word. When we are obediently following Jesus we will find that God takes care of our every need. If we are continually trusting in the world's system to provide for us, we are no longer trusting in God to supply for our needs. The world's system is broke and leads to destruction, but God's way of provision brings life and health and freedom. Our first most basic need is not for physical things as food, clothing, or shelter, but it is a spiritual need that is only met through having a committed relationship with God as the Lord over all areas of our life. As we trust in Him and live a life of righteousness, He will provide for our physical need for food, clothing, and shelter. He knows we have needs and He is ready to supply those need to us. We must simply trust Him and allow Him to be our source of provision. But, it is not without effort on our part that He meets our needs. We must work and not be lazy by expecting Him to provide for us while we sit around and do nothing. We must work and do as the Lord has told us in His Word. In 1 Timothy 5:8 we are told, *"But if anyone does not provide for his own, and especially for those in his household, he has denied the faith and is worse than an unbeliever."*

This verse is referring to food, shelter, and provisions we need to survive in this world. However, look at that verse again and read it as referring to spiritual matters. If we don't teach our children and family about the love of God we have found, then we are worse than an unbeliever who does not know God and, therefore, cannot teach his family of God's love.

First Timothy 5:8 is implying that we are to provide physical food, but we can also see how it is true that it can refer to feeding our families spiritual food. If we have family members who don't know God we need to stop being lazy and tell them about Him. Don't be shy or afraid to speak up. Since the Holy Spirit lives within us, He will guide us in ministering to them. We don't want to have regret someday after our loved one has passed away knowing we hadn't shared the saving grace of Jesus with them. What are you waiting for? Don't let them sleep the perpetual sleep and not know Christ. Wake them up to the love of God before they die. The scriptures say *today is the day of salvation*, so tell of the gift of salvation to your family and friends that they may accept Him as their Savior before it is too late.

> *"Seek the Lord while He may be found, Call upon Him while he is near."* Isaiah 55:6

> *"Behold, the Lord's hand is not shortened, that it cannot save; Nor His ear heavy, That it cannot hear."* Isaiah 59:1

Time is short and the year of the Lord's return is at hand. We need to examine our life and ask ourselves, "What have I done for the Lord?" This is the question we will need to answer when we stand before the Lord. What treasures did you store up in heaven? Have you served Jesus or have you served yourself? Have you helped the needy? Have you magnified the Lord before man, or have you magnified yourself?

This is the hour, this is the time, to rise up and awake from a carefree lifestyle. Look for ways to shine the light of God's glory so He may bring hope and healing to broken hearts. Jesus loves you with all of His being. He has been patient with you, but He is now warning you to wake up and make the changes in your life to live a devoted life for Christ. Be determined to answer His call. This doesn't mean that you are called to be a pastor or an evangelist. It simply means that God has called all of us to be His ministers and to bring His love and compassion to those who are lost in sin. And everyone who is born again through the blood of Jesus qualifies to fulfill that calling.

God doesn't need wish-washy Christians. He needs warriors who will stand up and fight the good fight of faith in the face of the adversity. When we are lazy in our service to Christ it is because we are giving into the flesh. Too much laziness and we sleep through our life with nothing of value to show on judgment day. You must wake up to the spiritual truth God has called you to. Stand up and speak boldly for His truth to set free those who are held captive in the bondage of sin.

One day we will be held accountable for knowing the truth and living by the truth, but not sharing the truth with others. We must speak up and not be ashamed of our faith nor be intimidated by what people may say or think. Jesus said, " *If you confess Me before man, then I will confess you before My Father in heaven; but if you do not confess Me, neither will I confess you before My Father in heaven*" (Matthew 10:32). If Jesus does not confess us before our Father in Heaven, then we will not be known by Him. On judgment day we would hear Him say, *"Depart from me, I never knew you"* (Matthew 7:22-23). Don't take that chance! Speak up for Him now that you may be called among them who will eternally live with Him.

God is warning us to wake up before we die. When our last breath is gone it will be too late to turn to Him. We have one chance to live and make things right with God and this is it. We have one chance to minister to the lost with the gospel, and this is it. Don't blow it! Don't waste your life on things that have no eternal value. Wake up before you die!

> *"...Now is the day of salvation."* 2 Corinthians 6:2c

> *"I am the way, the truth, and the life. No one comes to the Father except through Me."* John 14:6

> Heavenly Father,

> Thank You for being patient with me. Forgive me for not speaking out boldly for You. Give me the courage to say what You want me to say and to do what You want me to do. I desire not only to serve You, but to share the gospel with those who need to know You as their Lord and Savior. I ask for the Holy Spirit to give me greater boldness that I may shine a

light in this dark world for Your glory. Help me to not only love You, but to live as a warrior on fire with Your Word seared in my heart.

In Jesus' Name
Amen

"For I am not ashamed of the gospel of Christ, for it is the power of God to salvation for everyone who believes, …" Romans 1:16

"Most assuredly, I say to you, unless one is born again, he cannot see the kingdom of God." John 3:3

DAY 22

Where Is Your Focus?

> *"If then you were raised with Christ, seek those things which are above, where Christ is, sitting at the right hand of God. Set your mind on things above, not on things on the earth."* Colossians 3:1-2

What is your main focus in life? Do you focus on the positive or the negative events in your life? Do you focus on your needs or on meeting the needs of others? Do you care more about your present life than your eternal life? Who is number one in your life? Is it your children and family? Is it your job? Is it you or is it God?

Whatever occupies your mind is what holds your focus; and where your focus is held is from where you will reap a harvest. What you put your focus on grows and will produce after it's kind. If you think about good and produce good then you will reap that which is good. If your thoughts and words are evil then that is what you will reap. If you feel you have been having a string of bad luck, think back to what you have been focusing on. Many times we will find that we have been focusing on, and speaking, negative things over our life which is producing our harvest. There is a reason the Bible tells us to think on good things. Those things we think about will come forth from our lips. They have the power to either build us up or tear us down. Our thoughts and words have substance when we put them into action.

> *"Finally, brethren, whatever things are true, whatever things are noble, what ever things are just, whatever things are pure, whatever things are lovely, whatever things are of good report, if there be any virtue and if there is anything praiseworthy – meditate on these things."* Philippians 4:8

Our mouth will verbalize what our mind is focusing on. Our thoughts precede our words, therefore we know that we have been thinking negatively when we speak negative. If our mouth is expressing negative words we will reap negative things in our life. It is the God given law of sowing and reaping in action.

Our fleshly thinking can draw us into a negative thought pattern. It will take a determined effort to override the negative thoughts with positive thoughts. If we don't train our mind with the Word of God, our fleshly negative pattern of thinking will continue to lead us even after we have become a born again Christian. This is one reason it is important to read the Word of God daily. It will keep our mind thinking on positive things. We are living in a negative world whose god is Satan. Reading the Word helps us to focus on God, His love, and the blessings He has bestowed upon us instead of focusing on the world's empty chatter. When we live a positive life, we are sowing positive seeds into others and we reap positive in return. With the Word of God in our thoughts, we can live in this negative world and sow good into the lives of others. Remember that this world of sin and sorrow will pass away, but God's Word will last forever.

> *"So we do not focus on what is seen, but what is unseen. For what is seen is temporary, but what is unseen is eternal."* 2 Corinthians 4:18 HCSB

If you aren't sure where your main focus is ask yourself, "What is the most important thing to me today? What occupies most of my thoughts? What do I give most of my time towards?" The answer to those questions will reveal where your focus lies. If your thoughts are full of condemnation towards yourself and others then you have not completely turned over your thought life to God. When we turn over our thoughts to be inline with God our mind is renewed as we willingly seek to be transformed through His Word. When we are renewed in our mind, we will think good of ourselves and others, just as God does, and we will live with a positive attitude. The love of God will reach out to all people we come in contact with through our words and deeds.

> *"And do not be conformed to this world, but be transformed by the renewing of your mind, that you may prove what is the good and acceptable and perfect will of God."* Romans 12:2

The most important questions for you to ask yourself each day should always be, "What does God want me to do?" How can you serve Him greater and meet the needs of someone? How can you better fulfill the call God has placed upon your life? How can you reach at least one person with the gospel of Christ today in a way that will change their focus forever for the glory of God?

Notice that none of these questions focus on what you want to do, but instead they focus on what does God want you to do? This kind of self questioning takes the focus off of yourself and places it on God's priorities. His priority should always be our main focus. When you daily fulfill His plans instead of your plans, then you are dying to self a little more each day. We do this so we can become like Jesus as God's Word encourages us to do. As we ask God daily to lead us by His Holy Spirit we will be producing good fruit and making a difference for the kingdom of God. This is placing our focus on God and His priorities above all else.

> "*...be renewed in the spirit of your mind, and that you put on the new man which was created according to God, in true righteousness and holiness.*" Ephesians 4:23

Where is your focus? As Christians our focus should be on God and His purposes and plans. We must live a righteous life as we keep our eternal home in mind. By keeping that thought ever before us, we can better serve Him today. What we think and say and do each day will determine where we spend eternity. The Word of God must get into our mind and thoughts and be revealed though our actions and words. We grow in wisdom and understanding when we spend time studying the Word. The more we study the Word, the more we will think and speak like Jesus. With the Word fresh in us everyday we can keep our focus on that which is important to God. To maintain a godly focus about the world around us we must know what God says about it and what He desires us to do to change the world for Him. Don't allow the devil to distract you by entertaining the evil thoughts he tries to plant in your mind. Pondering on the negative thoughts wastes your time and opens the door for the devil to deceive you. Keep your focus on God and His Word so that you can live and think and speak inline with Him.

> *"For the word of God is living and powerful, piercing even to the division of soul and spirit, and of joints and marrow, and it a discerner of the thoughts and intents of the heart."* Hebrews 4:12
>
> Heavenly Father,
>
> I thank You for Your Word which keeps my focus on those things which concern You. I vow to keep my focus on You by seeking Your will first every day so I will fulfill the assignment You have set before me. May my words and thoughts and deeds be righteous and holy as I strive to bring hope to those around me while living in this negative world. Thank you for the many blessings you have given me. And thank You that I have a promised home in Heaven.
>
> In Jesus' Name
> Amen

"Do not be overcome by evil, but overcome evil with good." Romans 14:21

"Create in me a clean heart, O' God, and renew a steadfast spirit within me." Psalm 51:10

DAY 23

Entitlement

> *"He has not dealt with us according to our sins, nor punished us according to our iniquities."* Psalm 103:10

If God would give us exactly what we deserve, none of us would be here. By that I mean, because of our sin we deserve death, but Jesus paid the price for our sins on the cross. Without His sacrifice we would all be found guilty resulting in the penalty of death. God is being patient with mankind by offering ample time to turn from our wicked ways and come to Him. We are not entitled to anything, but God in His mercy has compassion on us, even while we were yet sinners.

The word *entitlement* conveys the right to guaranteed benefits, privileges, and claims; holding license, authority and legal access to certain advantages (according to Dictionary.com).

As born again believers we have certain rights bestowed on us through the death and resurrection of Jesus Christ. These entitlements are offered to everyone, but are not accepted by everyone. Acceptance is through acknowledging Jesus as Lord and Savior, and repenting of our sins. These benefits are warranted when the laws and stipulations that govern them are met. In order for these entitlements to be activated, we must live according to the Word of God.

> *"But the mercy of the Lord is from everlasting to everlasting on those who fear Him, and His righteousness to His children's children, to such as keep His covenant, and to those who remember His commandments to do them."* Psalms 103:17-18

The rights of a believer are available to he who believes, just as a driver's license is to a driver. When we meet the required age to drive we practice driving to receive our license. But we must pass the driving test requirements in our state to legally drive on the road. When we actually obtain the driver's license we must follow the rules of the road to keep our privilege to drive. We have an entitlement right to driving privileges, but these privileges can be taken away from us if we break the laws that govern the roadways. Our entitlement rights as a Christian have laws that govern them too.

We cannot say the sinners prayer to repent of our ways and then continue to live just as we had lived in our old sinful state. If our actions haven't changed, and our mouth hasn't changed, and our heart attitude hasn't changed, then our prayer of repentance was in word only. True repentance will bring a hunger to know God and His Word. As a believer we will seek Jesus with all of our heart. The hunger for more of God never leaves a true follower of Christ. After receiving salvation we grow in knowledge of all godliness from the Word which produces the fruit of righteousness. Without that deep hunger to know Him and reading the Word to feed our spirit, our commitment to follow Jesus will fade.

A born again believer who continues to seek God with a hungry heart has the rights and entitlements of an heir to the king. These rights and entitlements give us protection, health, wealth, blessings, peace, joy, power, and authority in the name of Jesus, (just to name a few). As we continue to grow in spiritual understanding by the Word of God, we produce all the fruit of the spirit mentioned in Galatians 5:22-23. *"But the fruit of the Spirit is love, joy, peace, long-suffering, kindness, goodness, faithfulness, gentleness, self-control..."* Christians are spiritually crucified with Christ and no longer have to accept the values of the world. Those who continue to live according to their flesh are not living in the full power of the Holy Spirit. They who do not grow in their understanding as a new believer are those who don't read the Word of God, or pray, or attend church services on a regular basis where the truth is being preached and therefore, they do not grow spiritually. Yet these people think they should have all the entitlements of a born again child of God because they call themselves Christians. They have an irrational sense of entitlement. An irrational sense of entitlement is when a person believes they deserve everything for doing nothing. If they are truly a Christian, they will speak, act, dress, work, behave, and love as a follower of Christ. They will continually grow in spiritual maturity which will be evident through their words and actions.

> *"Therefore, if anyone is in Christ, he is a new creation; old things have passed away; behold, all things have become new."* 2 Corinthians 5:17

> *"I am crucified with Christ: nevertheless I live; yet not I, but the Christ liveth in me; and the life which I now live in the flesh I live by the faith of the Son of God, who loved me, and gave himself for me."* Galatians 2:20 KJV

You have rights and privileges right now as a born again believer because in Heaven your name is written in the Lamb's Book of Life. This standing gives you all the rights as a citizen of Heaven, so you need to take authority over the devil and enjoy those benefits right now. Satan has no legal right to give you sickness, poverty or lack in any area of your life. Read the Word of God and know your entitlements as a faithful born again believer. Speak in line with the Word of God to keep your entitlement rights as a citizen of Heaven working in your behalf. When you speak in agreement with the devil you give authority to him and you walk away from your rights as a believer. Become fluent in the Word of God so that you will know your rights and authority as one who lives according to God's Word.

> *"For our citizenship is in heaven, from which we also eagerly wait for the Savior, the Lord Jesus Christ,..."* Philippians 3:20

Anyone choosing to live in sin has no legal rights to the entitlements provided to faithful believers of Christ. But when they repent and surrender their life to Christ, the gift of entitlements is theirs. As redeemed followers of Christ, we meditate daily in His Word in order to draw closer to Him and we grow in greater understanding of His will and His ways. We live with integrity revealing the love of God in all areas of life. Our life of love should point others to the way of salvation through Jesus, for it is by grace that we are all saved.

> *"For by grace you have been saved through faith, and not of yourself; it is the gift of God, not of works, lest anyone should boast."* Ephesians 2: 8-9

Do you want the entitlements of a believer to be active in your life? If so, you must surrender your life to Jesus. Are you a Christian, but you aren't seeing the benefits of living for God being manifested in your life? Then let me ask you, are you seriously seeking God and His will in every area of your life? Do you live in righteousness with right speaking, right attitudes, and right actions in every area?

You can draw closer to God by spending time in His Word and praying. You may need to ask God, "Where am I missing it, Lord?" When you earnestly seek Him, He will reveal things to you that you haven't completely given over to Him. No one is perfect, but we strive to be more like Christ by continually growing in knowledge and godly wisdom. God is not purposely hiding answers from us. He wants us to know His will in everything. Nothing is too big or too small to ask God to reveal His will to us in that area. He will often direct us to find the answer in His Word. "*Seek and you will find...*"(Luke 11:9). Never forget that His

Word is His will, and His will is His Word. If He says it in His Word, then you know that it is His will.

Today set your mind on the benefits of living for God as a faithful believer and live as a citizen of Heaven with all of it's advantages. Praise God that your sins are forgiven and for the privilege of being a citizen of Heaven. Live in your heavenly entitlement rights.

Heavenly Father,

Thank You for your Son Jesus who has rescued me from a life of sin, and thank You for the entitlement rights as Your child. I am so happy to be a citizen of Heaven with my name written in the Lambs Book of Life. I will diligently seek Your will in every area of my life as I live according to Your Word. I desire to stay close to You that I may never give up my rights to the devil with my words or actions. As I earnestly seek you, teach me through Your Holy Spirit what I need to know to successfully live according to Your Word. I give You all the praise and honor in all I do and say.

In Jesus' Name,
Amen

"And if you belong to Christ, then you are Abraham's descendants, heirs according to promise." Galatians 3:29

"But the Word is very near you, in your mouth and in your heart, that you may observe it." Deuteronomy 30:14

DAY 24

What Is Forever?

> *"The grass withers, the flower fades,*
> *But the word of our God stands forever."*
> Isaiah 40:8

The word '*forever*' comes up in our conversations often. We seem to say it rather loosely, even when we aren't really meaning that something is forever. Like we may say, "That took forever," or, "I waited for her forever,"or "This traffic light is taking forever." Let's see what forever really means? When we say something is lasting forever, we don't usually really mean forever.

Forever can mean always, endless and eternal. We may pledge our love to each other forever and a day. With this statement we are saying our love is endless, and eternal, and even beyond all of that. Is this even possible? We would like to hope so, but let's face it, we are human and our love can die with the passage of time. Many things pull on our affections and on our devotion to one another. Sometimes the pull is too great and the relationship ends. Our intentions were heartfelt and solid when we took our vows. But, in life there are no guarantees. Things change and people change. Our love isn't eternal, nor is it endless. Mankind may waver in feelings and dedication to another. I'm not saying there aren't people who fall in love at a young age, get married, and stay together throughout their lives. Their love gains strength through joy and trials that came their way. After forty plus years together, their love is still very strong. I have meet couples like that. My husband and I are counted among them. I thank God for the many years of the faithful love my husband and I share. Years ago, this type of commitment was normal, but in these days and times, it is unusual.

In contrast to human love, is the true undying love of God. He is not only eternal in His love, but He is eternal in every way. He is, He was, and He shall forever be. His Word is forever established and it will never change, nor will He. When He says He will love us forever, He will and He does. He is forever!

According to Dictionary.com other meanings of the word forever are infinite, permanent, continually, and never-ceasing. To use these descriptive words to explain God is right, but these same definitions do not accurately describe people. Since God is forever true and righteous, He is therefore, infinite, permanent, continual, and never-ceasing in His truth and righteousness. He never changes. God's Word tells us that, "*Jesus Christ is the same yesterday, today and forever*" (Hebrews 13:8). We know God's love toward us is eternal, for who would give their only son for anything that may be temporary?

> "*For God so loved the world, that He gave His only begotten Son, that whosoever believes in Him should not perish, but have everlasting life.*" John 3:16

We acknowledge that we are human and our feelings can change. And we have established that God is eternal and never changes. We need to understand that forever has no end, it is eternal, permanent, continual, and perpetually ongoing. Forever abides eternally unbroken, it is changeless and steadfast. We acknowledge forever to be beyond time as we understand it. And yes, God is all of that.

When we try to think of things that are forever, there are only a few things that are truly forever. One thing we know is that God is forever. "*I am the Alpha and the Omega, the Beginning and the End," says the Lord, "Who is and was and is to come, the Almighty*" (Revelation 1:8). God tells us that He is forever and He forever was. He has no beginning and He has no end. Also, there are many prayers recorded in the

Bible which convey the permanency of God. "*To Him who loved us and washed us from our sins in His own blood, and has made us kings and priests to His God and Father, to Him be glory and dominion forever and ever. Amen*" (Revelation 1: 5b-6). And then there's this one; "*Trust in the Lord forever, For in YAH, the Lord, is everlasting strength*" (Isaiah 26:4). We can only trust in a God that is forever. If He were here today and gone tomorrow, we would not dare to put our trust in Him. His steadfast eternal love would be discredited if His existence were temporary. But we know that God never changes; He is and forever shall be.

> "*Before the mountains were brought forth, or ever You had formed the earth and the world, even from everlasting to everlasting, You are God.*" Psalm 90:2

We also understand that His Word is forever. "*Forever, O Lord, your word is settled in Heaven*" (Psalm 119:89). Anything God said in His Word is for always and forever. His Word, just like Him, is forever. That is because God is His Word and His Word is God. Knowing this we can also discern that His will is forever. Because His Word is His will, and is His will is His Word. So we understand that God, and His will, and His Word, are all forever.

We can also add that that heaven is forever. According to Psalm 23:6; "*Surely goodness and mercy shall follow me all the days of my life and I will dwell in the house of the Lord forever.*" We will not live here on earth forever, but this verse say we are living in God's house forever, then heaven must be forever.

Another thing that is forever is our soul. Each time a soul is sent from heaven into a child forming in his mother's womb, from that time forward, that soul will live forever. When we die, our soul either goes to heaven to be with the Lord because our sins were washed under the blood of Jesus; or our soul goes to hell into the lake of fire for a life lived in sin without repenting. It is our choice where we will spend eternity. But one thing is for sure, our soul will live forever somewhere.

We have established that forever is a very, very long time. And that there are only a few things that are truly forever. These are God, His Word, His Will, Heaven and hell, and our soul. Everything else is temporary. There is a time and a season for all things, except for these. They are forever. So now here's the question. Where do you want to spend eternity? You have from now until you take your last breath to decide, but don't wait too long or it may be too late.

> *"But the mercy of the Lord is from everlasting to everlasting on those who fear him, And His righteousness to children's children, to such as keep his covenant, and to those who remember His commandments to do them."* Psalm 103:17-18

We have an invitation to spend forever in heaven with the Lord. Have you accepted that invitation yet?

> *"Let not your heart be troubled; you believed in God, believe also in Me. In My Father's house are many mansions; if it were not so, I would have told you. I go to prepare a place for you. And if I go and prepare a place for you I will come again and receive you to Myself; that where I am, there you may be also."* John 14:1-3

> *"... I am the way, the truth, and the life. No one comes to the Father except through Me."* John 14:6

It is only through Jesus that we can have a relationship with God the Father. As soon as we ask Jesus to forgive our sins and be our Lord and Savior, we have a promised home in heaven.

If you have never said that prayer and you would like to, repeat these words:

> *Heavenly Father,*
>
> *I come to You in the Name of Jesus. I ask You to come into my heart and be Lord over my life. I repent of my sins and I confess that Jesus is Lord. I believe Jesus lived a sinless life, died on the cross for my sins and that God raised Him from the dead. I believe Jesus is coming back again for me someday. Thank You Lord that I now have a new life in Christ and my sins are forgiven. I know according to John 14:1-3 that I have a promised home in Heaven as a new believer now and forever. In Jesus Name, Amen*

You are now a child of the Most High God with a new life in Christ. Read your Bible and become acquainted with God and His Word. By doing that you will grow in wisdom and knowledge of the ways of God. We start out as baby Christians, but as we continue to receive the Word of God into our thoughts our spirit begins to mature. Rest assured that every promise in the Bible is for you. Every word in the Bible is still alive and working for those who will tap into the treasures it holds. To God be all honor and glory!

Heavenly Father,

Thank You that we can spend forever with You both right now and in Heaven someday. And Thank You Lord that You never change. We can depend on You and Your love for us. What a blessing to be a new follower of Jesus. Help me to spiritually grow in all godly wisdom.

In Jesus' Name,
Amen

"*Most assuredly, I say to you, unless one is born again, he cannot see the kingdom of God.*" John 3:3

"*For Yours is the kingdom and the power and the glory forever. Amen.*" Matthew 6:4

DAY 25

Growing In Christ

> *"I don't mean to say that I have already achieved these things or that I have already reached perfection! But I keep working toward that day when I will finally be all that Christ Jesus saved me for and wants me to be."* Philippians 3:12 NLT

I can relate with these words Paul said. There are many things I write about that the Lord has taught me, but I certainly don't have them all mastered. The Holy Spirit teaches me through the Word as I study the scriptures. He gives me ideas and answers. He reveals His thoughts into my mind and shares His heart with me. As His message plays in my mind like a movie picture, I describe with written words what my mind sees and a story is born. I completely understand the message I was given, but I don't have the lesson mastered. I am in awe more than anyone as

I read over the contents of the stories I have written. I know it is through the anointing that I am able to write the stories, since even I, the one who penned the story, am able to learn from the message spoken into my spirit.

No one understands the Word of God so clearly that they have attained all they will ever need to know about God. We are all learning and growing in spiritual knowledge as we diligently seek to learn more of God. Everything we believe must always line up with the Word of God. If anyone tries to tell you something different than the truth of the Word, walk away from their teachings. Stand strong on God's Word and do not compromise. God's Word will never lead you astray. Man can waver, but God never does.

> *"God is not a man, that he should lie, nor a son of man, that he should change his mind."* Numbers 23:19a NIV

I went to a church some years ago that was forming in the town which I was living in at that time. In the beginnings of the church formation the worship was wonderful. As worship was sent up to God expectation grew in the heart of every believer. The pastor preached the truth of the Word with many scriptures to back up his teachings. God's Word was going forth and the small church quickly grew to over five hundred regular attenders within six months.

Departments were formed and leaders were assigned. This made age appropriate ministry available to everyone. It appeared that God was establishing something good. After about a year while working in the church office, I noticed the demeanor of the pastor had changed. At first it was only noticeable to those who worked closely to him, then it slowly began to come out in the words he said at the pulpit. It wasn't strong at first, but there was a little hint here and there that let us know our pastor was not staying connected with the Holy Spirit which alerted some of the church members that something was truly wrong. Eventually, everyone could tell the Spirit of God was being quenched, and the excitement of the services diminished more with each passing week. The prayer warriors noticed the change in the pastor and continually brought the situation before God. We knew in our spirit that something wasn't right, but we weren't exactly sure where the seed of the problem began. Then one day in prayer group it was revealed to us that the pastor had a spirit of greed. The anointing which had been so apparent at the beginning of the church formation was now gone.

Within the next few weeks the words of the pastor revealed his overconfidence in his ability to bring in the people. He began to think more highly of himself. He also had greater interest in the finances coming into the offerings than he did of the leading of the Holy Spirit, or the spiritual growth of the congregation.

The attendance of the church began to dwindle. Even I wondered where I should attend church since this minister was no longer delivering the truth of the Word. While I waited to hear from the Lord as to the direction I should take, it became very clear to me one Sunday morning while listening to the pastor preach. He blatantly said to the congregation, "I have attained perfection, though you need to continue to seek for it because you aren't there yet. I have grown in wisdom and knowledge of God and have acquired all I will ever need to know. You too can become perfect, like I am, if you will continue to come to church and hear me preach." The verse in the Bible, "*Do not be wise in your own eyes; Fear the Lord and depart from evil*" (Psalm 3:7), immediately came to my mind.

There it was! He elevated himself above the teachings of the Word of God and thought he was perfect in his understanding and wisdom. That was my cue to not just leave the church, but to quickly run as fast and as far away from his teachings as possible. I never stepped foot in that church again. But it wasn't just I however who left the church that day and never went back, many other people also left. Word got out that he was not preaching according to the Word of God. After about three months the church completely closed. Though it was not all a bad thing, because it spurred a core group of strong believers to form a new church in a different location. This new church had a wonderful anointing and grew by the power of the Holy Spirit. Today they are still going strong and teaching the full power of the Word of God.

The pastor from the old church had resigned and moved away. We later learned that he had a history of moving around the country and forming churches with the intent of gaining a following and financial gain from his preaching. The phrase comes to my mind, "beware of wolves in sheep clothing." That's just how he seemed to me and to all who had once been swayed by his enticing words.

I said all of that to say this. Never think that you have learned all there is to learn, or that you have attained perfection as a follower of Christ. There is always room to grow and a greater level to reach. When we start believing we have all the answers, we open the door to the enemy of our soul to deceive us by building up our ego. Magnifying self importance hinders our spiritual growth.

When the enemy begins to lie to you through someone you once believed to speak of the truth of God's Word, remember it is not that person we are fighting against. The enemy is working in that person. He is the one who is out to kill, steal, and destroy the Word of God that is in each of us.

> *"For we do not wrestle against flesh and blood, but against principalities, against powers, against rulers of the*

> *darkness of this age, against spiritual hosts of wickedness in the heavenly places."* Ephesians 6:12

To maintain a solid foundation in God's Word so that you will not be deceived, you must *read* God's Word. We grow in Christ by reading the Word daily, and by attending a faith based church where the full truth of the Word of God is preached. We have to renew our mind to think and act like Jesus. Obedience to that which we learn from the Word is the next step. If we learn all we can about God and His ways, and yet we do not put into practice that which we have learned, we will not grow spiritually. Just as faith without works is dead, it can also be said that learning without acting upon what we have learned fails to build spiritual muscle, and therefore, we will remain weak. Though we know the Word, and we believe the Word, if we don't act on the Word, we cannot get results from the Word. We are to *be doers and not merely hearers of the Word* (James 1:22).

> *"You see a man is justified by works and not by faith. For as the body without the spirit is dead, so faith without works is dead."* James 2:24,26

We mature spiritually by reading the Word, by listening to the Word preached, and by acting on that which we have learned. As we follow these steps in our spiritual walk we will gain understanding of the deeper things of God. The Holy Spirit is a wonderful teacher who knows just how much to reveal to you and He knows when you are ready for more. Allow Him to show you the treasures of the Word as you daily seek to grow in deeper understanding and wisdom in all godliness. Stay connected to God and let nothing (and no one) separate you from Him.

> *"Abide in Me, and I in you. As the branch cannot bear fruit of itself, unless it abides in the vine, neither can you, unless you abide in Me."* John 15:3-4

The pastor in my story became disconnected with Jesus, who is the vine, which caused his downfall. Just as I must always be listening for the messages the spirit brings to me and be obedient in writing accurately that which He tells me, so must we all be listening and ready to act upon His words. It is through our obedience to the Spirit that we disclose our spiritual maturity. Our actions, words, and deeds manifest the depth of our devotion and obedience to God. If we find that we are not growing in Christ, we need to reevaluate our life and be sure we are putting Him first. And if other things are distracting us from our dedication to becoming all that God had planned for us, we need to repent and prioritize our commitments. Follow the steps it takes to grow in

Christ and see what wonderful things God will do through you.

> *"Trust in the Lord with all your heart, and lean not on your own understanding; In all your ways acknowledge Him, and He shall direct your path."* Psalm 3:5-6

Heavenly Father,

Thank You for teaching me through the Holy Spirit and for being patient with me as I learn. Your Word is my instruction manual where I gain spiritual wisdom and understanding. Remind me to go to Your Word for answers and not to simply take the word of others. I know all teaching must match up with Your Word in order to be truth. Thank you that I can trust in You at all times to keep me on the right path. Help me to always be sensitive to the Holy Spirit as He teaches me and helps me to grow in all spiritual wisdom.

In Jesus' Name,
Amen

> *"And whoever exalts himself will be humbled, and he who humbles himself will be exalted."* Matthew 23:12

"A disciple is not above his teacher, nor a servant above his master." Matthew 10:24

"Do not be wise in your own eyes; fear the Lord and depart from evil. It will be health to your flesh, and strength to your bones." Proverbs 3:7-8

DAY 26

Are You His Friend?

"A friend loves at all time." Proverbs 17:17 NKJ

There's a song with the lyrics that say, 'I am a friend of God, He calls me friend', it has a catchy tune. But can we truthfully sing these words if it is not true? We know God is a friend to all who trust in Him, but are we being a real friend to Him? Do we really treat Him as a friend? Do we really trust in Him? Are we concerned about what He thinks and what He has to say? What is a friend and how is a friendship suppose to look? What keeps friendship alive? What does friendship with God look like?

Here are some definitions Dictionary.com gives for what a friend is: 'a person attached to another by feelings of affection or personal regard; a person who gives assistance or support; a person who is on good terms with another; a person who is not hostile.'

And for the word friendship it defines it as having a friendly relationship.

As a friend to someone we are to value them; who they are, what they like and don't like and we enjoy their character and personality. We will communicate with a friend often and we want to spend time with them. The more we spend time together, the stronger our friendship grows. Have you ever tried to be a friend to someone who doesn't seem to want to be your friend? When you try to talk to them they shut you out and ignore you. Or even worse, they walk away when they see you coming. You show them kindness as you continually reach out to them, but your kind gestures are not received or returned. That hurts!

Now can you imagine how Jesus feels when He gave His all for you and yet you refuse to be His friend? His friendship offers us what no other friendship is able to, it offers the redemption of sin and eternal life. God reaches out to us through the pages of His Word. As we read the Bible we get to understand His character not only as Lord and Savior, but as a friend. We learn to communicate with Him as someone who is concerned about our everyday situations just as any friend should be. A friend takes time to call on you and they will help you whenever you are in need. And a friend will love you no matter what mood you are in. That's what Jesus is to us. He is that friend who calls on us, helps us and loves us unconditionally. But it is up to us to answer His call. Without our response to His invitation to be His friend Jesus will not insist that we accept His offer. He is gentle and kind and desires our friendship, and He patiently waits for us to acknowledge Him as our friend. He never forces Himself on anyone. It is to our advantage to be a friend to Jesus. The benefits of His friendship assist us in our every day life. He listens to our complaints and counsels us. He comforts our heart when we are grieving. We can talk to Him any hour of the day or night and He is always ready to listen. He gives us rest when we are weary. He is with us in times of trouble. And when we feel lonely He sends someone our way to let us know He cares. His rules for our friendship are few. He simply want to hear from us and for us to communicate with Him.

> *"A man who has friends must himself be friendly..."* Proverbs 18:24a

To be a friend we must act like a friend. A friend to Jesus will desire to spend time with Him. If we don't read the Bible, and we don't pray, and we don't listen to His Word preached, then we don't really know Him and we are not His friend. Friendship is a two way street. We are not to only pray when we want something from Him. We don't like it when someone only remembers that we are their friend when they want something from us. And we cannot expect someone to be a friend to us when we are unfriendly to them. But Jesus never rescinds His offer to be our friend. Jesus wants to talk with us, to laugh with us, and to share our good times and our bad times, just because He loves us, and that's what friends do.

Have you ever heard that it gets lonely at the top? I wonder how Jesus feels. Once I heard a minister say Jesus told him that 'He was lonely and that He wants a friend.' He is the King above all kings and He is all power, and yet He desires to have a personal relationship with us. That tells me that friendship to Him is very important. A one-on-one relationship with Jesus is what He desires from every believer.

Do you know Jesus as your friend? Do you get up in the morning and say, "Good morning Jesus," as if He were sitting there waiting for you to get up? Do you talk to Him throughout your day? If your relationship with Jesus is not on a friendship basis yet, I suggest that you begin to draw closer to Him and allow Him to be your best friend. You will see that the more time you spend talking to Jesus, as you would a friend who is right by your side, that you will have greater peace and joy in your life. We all need a friend to talk to. Talk to Jesus about everyday situations in your life. He will carry your burdens and lighten your load, and He will guide you with each decision you need to make. You can confide in Him as a friend about everything.

I have found it comforting to talk with the Lord as I go about my day. He brings me peace in an otherwise rushed day. And on those days that I seem to have a lot of extra alone time, He is my companion who is always near. With Jesus as my personal friend I am never alone.

> *"Nevertheless I am continually with You; You hold me by my right hand."*
> Psalm 73:23

> Heavenly Father,

> Thank You for always being by my side. You are a friend that I can count on and trust in. It is good to know You not only want to be my Lord, but You also want to be my friend. Thank You for Your love and patience with me through my good days and my bad days. I am so grateful You call me friend. I will build on our relationship through prayer, praise, reading Your Word, and visits with You. Thank You for being my Lord and Savior, and personal friend.

> In Jesus' Name
> Amen

> *"I will never leave you nor forsake you."*
> Hebrews 13:5

"*...I am with you always, even to the end of the age.*" Matthew 28:20b

"*...The sweetness of a man's friend gives delight by hearty counsel.*" Proverbs 27:9b

DAY 27

But God...

> *"For indeed he was sick almost unto death;* ***but God*** *had mercy on him..."*
> *Philippians 2:27*

God will intervene in any situation you give over to Him. Believe with the faith that moves mountains as you seek His will to come to pass according to His purpose and plan. There are numerous stories in the Bible when God came into the picture and turned the situation around. He took a bad situation and made it good. He will take your sorrow and give you joy. No matter what the circumstances are, if you will completely give it over to God and walk in faith, He will bring you out on the other side with joy. To live in His blessings and mercy we cannot fall away from our faith in God because of temporary circumstances. And everything is temporary if you give it to God. Don't get stuck in the land of "*what am I going to do*?" No! Stand in faith and know the Bible says, ***but God.***

> *"Therefore, consider God's kindness and severity; severity towards those who have fallen,* ***but God****'s kindness toward you ... if you remain in His kindness..."*
> Romans 11:22 HCSB

When you feel depressed because of circumstances in your life that you can't seem to change, know God will lift you up. When you get a bad report from the doctor, know God is your healer. When your bank account is overdrawn and you don't know how you will make it through another week, know God is your supply. Know in every situation that God will come through for you. The Bible says, *"but God* "showed up and changed the outcome. Never despair because of a negative report. Instead, know it is an opportunity to stand in faith and see God come through for you in a miraculous way.

Paul was in prison ***but God*** showed up and caused an earthquake which allowed the prison gates to open. *"Suddenly there was a great earthquake, so that the foundations of the prison were shaken; and immediately all the doors were opened and everyone's chains were loosed"* (Acts 16:26). Paul's situation looked hopeless but when he prayed, God showed up.

And in another bible story we read about when Jesus was laid in the tomb a large stone was placed over the door, the tomb was sealed and guards were positioned beside it. All hope seemed to be lost for Jesus' followers, ***but God*** sent a great earthquake and *"an angel of the Lord descended from heaven, and came and rolled back the stone from the door, and sat on it"* (Matthew 27:60, 66; 28:3).

God can take hopeless situations and turn them around for His glory.

> *"But God has chosen the foolish things of the world to put to shame the wise, and God has chosen the weak things of the world to put to shame the things which are mighty."* 1 Corinthians 1:27

When a difficult situation comes my way, and I have no answer to resolve it, I know I can pray for God to intervene. As I stand firm on His promises, He moves on my behalf giving me the victory. I quote the words, ***'but God'*** many times during trials. We have to pray, hold our peace and believe. God will always do what He says He will do. If you can find scriptures in His Word to back up your request then you know you'll receive the answer. God does not, and cannot, lie. He will fulfill every promise He has made to us in His Word if we will only believe. Pray His Word back to Him and stand on His promises.

I recently received a negative report from my doctor. To the world the condition was incurable, but not for

God. Arthritis must bow it's knees to the Name of Jesus just like all other diseases must do. It was just another opportunity for God to show up and turn the situation around. After the doctor said his piece, I said '***But God***!' Because I know God can do what doctors can't do. When I do my part and stand in faith after giving the problem over to God, He will turn the bad report into a good report. I even had a doctor change His mind about a condition I once had when he could no longer find the illness in my body anywhere. The doctor said, "I'm going to take multiple sclerosis off your chart." Yup! It was another ***but God*** thing! Hallelujah! God is the only one who has the final say in your life if you will allow Him to. Your doctors report is not the end of the story, nor is your negative bank statement the end of the story. Who are you going to allow to determine the outcome of each situation in your life, God or man?

> "*Who hath believed our report? And to whom is the arm of the Lord revealed?*
> Isaiah 53:1

Negative reports should not move you if you are walking in faith and believe what the Word of God says. I learned from a wonderful minister to speak to the negative report by saying, "I'm not moved by what I see, I'm not moved by what I hear, I'm not moved by what I feel. I'm only moved by the Word of God and the Word of God says I am healed." Since I have learned to do this it is now easier to walk in faith and watch my victory come.

So next time you are faced with an impossible situation just remember the Bible tells us many times, ***but God***! Ask God for His help. Believe He will intervene on your behalf as you stand in faith, and watch God move mountains for you. ***But God*** will come through for you every time!

> *"Yet in all these things we are more than conquerors through Him who loved us."*
> Romans 8:37

> Heavenly Father,
>
> I know I can trust You to turn each negative report around that I may face when I give it to You. Thank You for changing the a bad report into a report of victory. You have the answer to every situation and I know as I trust in You that You will turn bad news around for my benefit and for Your glory. Help me to always stand in faith when trials come. I'm not moved by what I see, feel, or hear. I'm only moved by the Word of God. And Your Word says, *by His stripes I am healed, and nothing is impossible*

with God. Thank You Lord, I stand on this.

In Jesus' Name
Amen

"That your faith should not be in the wisdom of men but in the power of God." 1 Corinthians 2:5

"But my God shall supply all your need according to His riches in glory by Christ Jesus." Philippians 4:19

"Not by might nor by power, but by My Spirit, says the Lord of hosts." Zechariah 4:6

DAY 28

Judging Yourself Harshly

"I have not departed from your judgment, for You Yourself have taught me." Psalms 119:102

As a child of God we have a desire to please Him. We want to do our best and give our best in service to God. Scriptures tell us we are to love our fellow believer as we love God. In showing our love for others, we need to do our best and give our best in obedience to the Word. We are to love others as God loves us. If we love someone, we will do for them, meaning we help them, and we are kind and caring towards them. We do this willingly with a servant's attitude because of the love we have for God which leads us into serving others. We give our all to God and to others.

So why has giving your all not been enough? Do you push yourself to do more? Do you feel guilty all the time because you think you should do more for the church, more for the brethren, more for your family, or more for God? But what does God's Word say we are to do?

The Word of God says we are to, "*...love the Lord your God with all our heart, with all of your soul, with all of your strength, and with all of your mind, and your neighbor as yourselves*" (Luke 10:27). God's command is for us to love Him and to love each other, but He will not push us to fulfill that commandment. Loving others is simply a natural part of loving Him. If we love God, we will love people. That is Christian love in action.

God does not require you to do everything that others want you to do. Trying to please everyone will wear you out and leave you feeling overwhelmed. The push you feel to do more is not from God. God will not push anyone into doing anything. His Spirit is gentle, not pushy. The Spirit of God inside of you will nudge you toward the path God has for you, but it will not be with a forceful nag or push. If what you think you should do feels dreadful, tormenting, or pushy, you can be sure it's not from God.

> *"Come to Me all who labor and are heavy laden, and I will give you rest. Take my yoke upon you and learn from Me, for I am gently and lowly in heart, and you will find rest for your soul. For*

My yoke is easy and My burden is light."
Matthew 11:28-30

There are three main sources that pressure us to do more; Satan, self, and people.

Satan always wants you to think that you don't measure up to the standard of a dedicated servant of God. He wants you to become so discouraged in your efforts to be a better Christian that you eventually give up and walk away from your faith. Don't let him push you out of the blessings God has for His faithful children. This is where you put into action the scripture that tells us to *'resist the devil and he will flee,'* (James 4:7). We cannot afford to listen to the lies of the devil. Any suggestion he gives you is a clue that you need to do the opposite, because *he is a liar and the father of lies* (James 8:44), and does not have truth in him. His purpose is *to kill, steal, and destroy,* (John 10:10). We need to be established in the Word of God so we will be wise to the schemes of the devil. God's Word will put a witness in your spirit to unveil any hidden agenda that Satan has for you.

Self constantly compares you against the success of others. Self, which is flesh, tells you that you aren't serving in the church enough, or that you aren't helping others as much as you should. Self will lead you to believe that you can become more important to others and the church if you would only do more.

Your flesh says you need to work harder to measure up to the standards of the church to be a better giver, a better servant, and a more dedicated believer. Flesh will wear you out trying to do more and be more than God ever called you to do or be. God does not want us to do anything we were not called to do. When we get into pleasing the flesh, we place ourselves in areas of ministry that we know nothing about. It is not up to us to decide where we want to minister. That is God's job. He will tell you where *He* wants you to work when you ask Him. As born-again Christians, Jesus can motivate us to live responsible, Christlike lives faithfully fulfilling the call God has given us. Rely on God, not on your flesh.

People may try to make you feel guilty because they believe all followers of Christ should spend most of their time helping out in the church or volunteering in the community. They don't take into account that you may have already talked to God about this and you are doing what you believe He has told you to do. They may say things to you that hurt you in their efforts to stir you up to do what they think you should do. Yet, in their condemnation of you, they are hurting themselves each time they strike out with unkind words. In judging you they are showing lack of good Christian character. We are not to judge our fellow believers. We are to support one another and love them. Let God do His job in stirring up someone to do what He has called them to do.

"There is therefore now no condemnation to those who are in Christ Jesus, who do not walk according to the flesh, but according to the Spirit." Romans 8:1

If you are feeling pressured to do more, to get more involved, to be more of a helper, to reach out more, and serve more, then maybe it's time that you let go of all the pressures and get alone with God. The push is not from God. We have already established that God's Spirit is gentle and He will never push you to do anything. We have a free will because God wants us to be free to decide to follow the leading of the Holy Spirit, or to follow our own path. If we had a pushy God, He would not have given us free will. He would have forced us to serve Him, but He doesn't. We get to choose. However, we are to be busy working for the Lord. We cannot sit around and expect others to do the assignment God has called us to do. Follow the leading of the Holy Spirit who will put you on the right path as to where you are to work in service unto the Lord.

> *"Choose for yourself this day whom you will serve ..... But as for me and my house, we will serve the Lord."* Joshua 24:15

Let go of all the worry and cares of doing more. Get alone with God. Get your Bible, a pen, and paper, and spend time alone with God. Talk to Him. Tell Him how you feel and what you think. Ask Him to reveal to you what He wants you to do. He will let you know if there are things you are doing that you are to let go of. And He will reveal to you if there are areas He wants you to work in where you are not yet involved. Trust the Holy Spirit to lead you into the right ministry. He may even lead you into a whole new area of service.

What God wants for you is all that matters. It makes no difference what your flesh wants to do, or what Satan wants you to do, or what others want you to do. What matters is what God wants. How can He use you? Discover where God wants you to work and do it! Then when you feel the push coming against you again, check with God to be sure you haven't gotten off track from the assignment He has given to you. Listen only to God and follow Him. His Spirit will never lead you down the wrong path; you can always depend on Him to keep you on the right track.

> "*Make me to walk in the path of Your commandments, for I delight in it.*"
> Psalms 119:35

You can judge yourself harshly when you listen to anything other than the voice of God. Harsh self-judgment will make you feel defeated no matter how much you do for God and others. Stop listening to those voices. Tune in your ears to only the voice of God. His Spirit will gently direct your steps on the journey He has for you. When you know in your heart that you are following His leading the overwhelming feeling of defeat will be replaced with calm peace in your soul. Remember, there is only one voice you should be listening to, and that is the voice of God. Tune in your listening ear to receive His station only. All other stations are just fuzzy background noise. Don't take the time to tune into their chatter, they are only attempting to distract you from the voice of God.

> *"My son, give attention to my words; Incline your ear to my sayings."* Proverbs 4:20

Are you feeling pressured to do more than you believe God wants you to do? Are you confused by too many voices telling you what to do? You need to stay in God's Word and continually be in communication with Him. Allow His Spirit to direct you according to His plan and purpose for your life. Then when negative pressures come, you will recognize them for what they really are and they will not distract you from the path God has placed you on.

> *"My sheep hear My voice, and I know them, and they follow Me."* John 10:27

Heavenly Father,

I thank You that I can trust in Your Spirit to lead me and guide me according to Your plan and purpose for me. Help me to close out the distractions that try to push me into doing things You have not assigned me to do. Forgive me for comparing myself with others. Thank You for the ministry You have given to each one who serves You. Help me to love my fellow brethren and not to judge them nor judge myself harshly. You are my hiding place. In You I stand equipped to do the work You assign me to do.

In Jesus' Name,
Amen

"But he who is joined to the Lord is one spirit with Him." 1 Corinthians 6:17

"If we live in the Spirit, let us also walk in the Spirit. Let us not become conceited, provoking one another, envying one another." Galatians 5: 25-26

"For it is God who works in you both to will and to do for His good pleasure." Philippians 2:13

DAY 29

The Voice of A Thankful Heart

"But thanks be to God, who gives us the victory through our Lord Jesus Christ."
1 Corinthians 15:57

When the Holy Spirit inspired me to write this message, He impressed on me that we must first erase complaining and criticizing from our lips if we are to ever live in His blessings. When we complain or criticize we do not reflect a thankful heart. Being thankful and yet complaining speaks opposite of each other. If we say we are thankful, but we complain and criticize, we are saying one thing and doing another. The Bible tells us that praising God with our mouth and complaining from that same mouth isn't acceptable. We are either a complainer or we are one who gives praise, we are one or the other. We cannot be on both sides of the fence at the same time. We need to crucify the spirit of complaining that comes from our unrepented flesh. Our lips praise God, but our complaining cancels out that praise. The Bible calls it talking with a forked tongue. We are to walk in love as believer's, and in order to do that, the words we use must be loving, kind, and come from a thankful heart. The words we speak must always line up with the Word of God.

> *"Out of the same mouth proceed blessing and cursing. My brethren, these things ought not to be so."* James 3:10

A thankful heart allows us to see value in all things, great or small, that come into our life. When we are thankful, we edify and lift up. When we complain or criticize we are mocking and tearing down with words that destroy ourselves and others. We not only degrade what we are complaining about, but we also degrade ourselves with our negative attitude. Our words are our witness. If we confess to be a Christian, what type of witness is it to others when we complain and criticize? As Christians we are to live with joy in our heart and be thankful for all God has done for us. A joyful and thankful heart is a good witness to those around us. A thankful heart builds up and does not destroy.

> *"A joyful (thankful) heart does good like a medicine."* Proverbs 17:22

We won't be displaying a joyful or thankful heart if we practice complaining and criticizing. When we become students of the Word of God our mind is renewed. Those things we once complained about become less annoying to us as we continue to learn how to deal with differences according to God's Word. It is the old fleshly nature in us that wants to complain and criticize, but when our mind is renewed we begin to think in line with the Word of God. God's thoughts become our thoughts about each situation that arises.

> *"And do not be conformed to this world, but be transformed by the renewing of your mind, that you may prove what is that good and acceptable and perfect will of God."* Romans 12:2

Do you need to have something to be thankful for? Then think about how God loves you so much that He gave His only son to die on the cross for your sins. That is something worthy of being thankful for. Nothing else that happens in your life is as amazing as that one act of love. Your complaining attitude is as filthy rags when it is compared to the suffering of the cross. While we were yet sinners, God had compassion on us by displaying His grace and mercy toward us. If we received what we really deserved, we would have no hope of redemption and we would be bound for hell. But, thanks be to God for His compassion towards us which He lovingly demonstrated through the death and resurrection of His Son Jesus, that we may receive the promise of eternity through Him. Not only do we have redemption from our sins, but we are delivered from the power of the darkness and transformed into the kingdom of light. And when we make mistakes and repent, we can thank God that we will be forgiven and restored through Him. Hallelujah! Now that is something to be extremely thankful for!

> "*Since we are receiving a kingdom that cannot be shaken, let us be thankful, and so worship God acceptably with reverance and awe.*" Hebrews 12:28 NIV

We will experience many blessings when we live with a thankful heart. The voice of a thankful attitude lifts us above the trials that come against us when we are living a life of faith. Being thankful for who we are in Christ, no matter what comes our way, denies the devil access to our thought life where he tries to cause confusion and doubt. When we no longer yield to the lies of the devil, and we have learned to stand on the solid truth of the Word, we cannot be shaken. The backbone of thankfulness supports faith. If you confess unshakable faith, you will live with a thankful heart, you will exhibit a thankful attitude, and you will humbly exalt the Lord through expressions of a heart filled with praise.

When we pray, we are to believe that we have whatever we prayed for and thank God for the answer even before we see the answer physically manifested. As we believe for the answer, our thankful attitude reveals our faith in God. "*...Have faith in God. For assuredly, I say to you, whoever says to this mountain be removed and be cast into the sea, and does not doubt in his heart, but believes that those things he says will be done, he will have whatever he says,"* (Mark 11:22-23). We must stand firm and believe for the answer to our prayers. Do not doubt or talk against what you had prayed for. Our heart of thanksgiving and praise reveals our faith in God to answer our request.

With the confessions of our lips we convey a thankful heart. Our words are to be pure and uplifting and spoken with love. This is how a thankful heart sounds. This is the voice of a thankful heart. If you have a problem in this area, ask God to help you to change your attitude from complaining, to an attitude of being thankful. Be determined to live with the voice of a thankful heart.

> *"Therefore by Him let us continually offer the sacrifice of praise to God, that is, the fruit of our lips, giving thanks to His name."* Hebrews 13:15

Heavenly Father,

I come to You today and ask You to forgive me for complaining and criticizing. I ask for Your help to change my attitude from one which tears down, to one which builds up. When I see or hear something that I used to complain about, remind me to keep my mouth shut and give it to You. Help me to find things throughout my day to be thankful for. Help me as I go through this process of changing my heart and attitude from complaining and criticizing to being joyful and thankful. I desire to live with a thankful heart and speak words of thanksgiving.

In Jesus' Name,
Amen

"And whatever you do in word or deed, do all in the name of the Lord Jesus, giving thanks to God the Father through Him." Colossians 3:17

DAY 30

Addicted to God

> *"You shall love the Lord your God with all your heart, with all your soul, with all your strength, and with all your mind, and your neighbor as yourself."*
> Luke 10:27

There is a secular song from some years ago that says, "I'm addicted to love." As Christians we know that God is Love. So we should all be able to say, "I'm addicted to God." If you are a Christian addicted to God you will continually hunger for Him. A passionate follower of Jesus will press forward as he endures trials and breaks through every barrier that Satan puts in front of him. Each challenge makes the believer stronger in their resolve to stay on the path God has set before them.

When we are addicted to God we have a driving passion to serve God. Our heart is open to each new area where we will grow in our understanding and wisdom of spiritual matters. God will remind us of attitudes we have that need to be changed, even when we don't think it needs to change. But, if we are really hungry for God, and we are addicted to Him and His love, we will surrender to His will and follow wherever He leads. Many things in life seem to be a test and if we love God, and the people God brings into our life, we will pass the test. It is all based on love. Everything in God's kingdom hinges on love. There are difficult people in our lives who will sharpen and elevate us to the place where God wants us to be. But that means we must be willing to forgive them and die to envy, pride, judgmental attitudes and selfishness. The death of these fleshly ways are a necessary step of dying to self. When we love God we will love people, just as He does. As iron sharpens iron, so does an irritating person sharpen us spiritually.

I learned many years ago that the more I learn about God there is so much more I don't know about Him. If we study His Word day and night, and if we listen to the great preachers of past and present, and though we seek to know and do His will, we will never completely *know* Him. God is so great and mighty in all of His ways that it is too high for human understanding. However, in our diligence to seek Him, we gain spiritual understanding that elevates us up to a new level of faith and trust in Him. Searching to understand Him deeper keeps our eyes on the pages of His Word and off of the distractions of this world. Our hunger for more of God will lift us above our own understanding and set us on a plain where we can attain more of Him in our life.

I hunger after God. It is a love for God that never leaves me from wanting more of Him. I live a life addicted to God, seeking His will and His ways with the purpose of knowing His incomparable glory and His power. When life is lived addicted to Him we seek Him more than anything else in life; His beauty, His love, and His compassion are magnified. With each new revelation He unfolds to me, another depth of His character is revealed, and I am exhilarated with a deeper understanding of Him. As my spiritual understanding grows God grants me more boldness and power to reach the world with the good news of His love.

Everyone is addicted to something. Some people are addicted to sports. Others are addicted to TV, or movies, or music. There are addictions that Satan puts on people that become vices and are difficult to break, like drinking or smoking or illegal drugs. But none of these addictions will give eternal joy; they are empty with no eternal value. Those ungodly addictions that consume people will drag them to hell someday if they don't repent and turn to God while there is still time. I know this sounds harsh, but the Word of God tells us to seek Him while He may be found. We will all be judged for what we have done with our life. If we waste it on empty pleasures we will have nothing of value to show for our life when we stand before the Throne of Judgment, and we will hear, "*Depart from Me, I never knew you*" (Matthew 7:23). The only addiction that will stand worthy of a life well lived is the addiction we have for more of God. As we allow God to use us to further His kingdom and we abide in His presence daily, we are storing up treasures in Heaven. Then we will hear on judgment day, "*Well done My good and faithful servant*" (Matthew 25:21). That's what I desire to hear. How about you?

We are to love all people and share the love of Jesus with them while there is still time. In Ezekiel 33:7-9 we are warned that if we do not warn the lost to turn from their evil ways, and they die in their sin, their blood will be on our hands. But if we tell them of Jesus' saving grace but they refuse to accept His love and forgiveness, then our soul will be saved. It is the job of all of us who believe the Word of God to share it with everyone. If we love others the way God loves them we will be eager to share the good news. When we live addicted to God and His love we long to see others receive His mercy and His grace just as we have. Remember, Christ died for everyone!

> "*But sanctify the Lord God in your hearts, and always be ready to give*

> *a defense to everyone who ask you a reason for the hope that is in you with meekness and fear."* 1 Peter 3:15

The love of God is forever because God is forever. To be addicted to God is to always strive to please Him in all we do and say. When we strive to please Him we will be obedient to His call and allow Him to lead our steps. To be addicted to God is to abide in His presence and to crave to know Him greater. We will hunger to know more of Him through His Word. Keeping ourselves pure and righteous as a living vessel that may be used for the glory of God is the duty of every believer. We should *always* be hungry for more of Him.

> *"Meditate on these things; give yourself entirely to them, that your progress may be evident to all... For in doing this you will save both yourself and those who hear you."* 1 Timothy 4:15-16

> *"I spread out My hands to You; My soul longs for You like a thirsty land."* Psalm 143:6

Diligently seek Him and you can say, *"He is the glory and the lifter of my head* (Psalm 3:3). *He is the light of the world* (John 8:12). *He is my strength and my song* (Exodus 15:2). *He is my joy and my delight* (Psalm 43:4). *He is my shepherd* (Psalm 23:1). *He satisfies my thirst* (Rev 21:6; John 4:13-14). Jesus is my all in all. There is no one like God. How blessed I am to belong to the family of God."

> "*Set your mind on things above, not on things on the earth.*" Colossians 3:2

Are you in love with Jesus? Do you crave to know God in a deeper way? Have you become addicted to His love yet? Allow God to reveal Himself to you through the pages of His Word. When we hunger for God with all our heart He will fill us with His wisdom and His love in overflowing abundance. Let the depth of His love and mercy overflow in you and through you. The peace and joy you will find in Him is far more precious than gold. Lived addicted to God!

> "*Blessed are those who hunger and thirst after righteousness for they shall be filled.*" Matthew 5:6

> Heavenly Father,
>
> Fill me to overflowing with Your Spirit and Your love that I may be equipped to share the good news of Your mercy. I seek to know You more and to gain greater wisdom and understanding of Your ways. I give my time, my resources, and my talents to Your service. May I always be obedient to Your instructions

that You will find me worthy of your calling. I ask that You reveal Yourself to me in a greater way as I dig deeper in Your Word. I hunger and thirst for more of You Lord. I desire to live addicted to You and only You.

In Jesus' Name,
Amen

"My soul thirsts for God, the living God." Psalm 42:2a

"Be diligent to present yourself approved to God, a worker who does not need to be ashamed, rightly dividing the word of truth." 2 Timothy 2:15

"Let us hold fast to the confession of our hope without wavering, for He who promised is faithful." Hebrews 10:23

DAY 31

God Understands

> *"... for the Lord searches all hearts and understands all the intents of the thoughts...."* 1 Chronicles 28:9b

Did you ever say something and the words got turned around? Like, "I showered yesterday evening and mowed my hair after I washed the grass." Yup! I said that. But do you know I meant to say, "I showered and washed my hair yesterday evening after I mowed the grass?" Yes, I thought so. You knew what I was trying to say didn't you? Though jumbled up words get a laugh, when the words come out in the wrong order, the hearer usually knows what we are trying to say. Our text messages can get scrambled too. A cell phone can get tricky when you text if your auto correct is activated on your phone. It can put words in your text that you don't want to say. I have learned to check what the auto correct thinks I want to say (usually) before I send the text. There have been some very strange words auto correct has selected for me. The receiver of the text generally knows what you are saying even when auto correct sends strange words to them in your message, at least those who really know you usually understand what you are saying. That's the way it is with God. He knows us and He understands what we are saying even when our words are mixed up and out of order.

At those times when we have something on our heart, but when we attempt to tell Jesus about it the words get all jumbled up, we can rest assured that He understands what we are saying. Someone told me once that I pray pretty prayers. I'm not sure what she was referring to but we don't have to pray a pretty prayer for God to understand our heart. The Scripture says, *'He understands the intent of our thoughts'* (1 Chronicles 28:9). Which means He knows what we are trying to say and He understands our intention. He sees our heart of compassion for a lost loved one, or our broken heart over a sad situation. He knows our needs and our desires. He knows what we are going through and what we want to say even before there is one word on our lips. We simply need to come to Him with an open heart and let Him know our desire for Him to meet our need. God in His mercy and compassion for us leans down His ear and listens to our hearts cry. Though there may be thousands of prayers ascending up to the heavenly throne at that exact time, He will stop and listen intently to you, because you are that important to Him. He wants to hear from you and bless you. He is waiting to hear you call to Him.

> *"If you bide in Me, and My words abide in you, you will ask what you desire, and it shall be done for you."* John 15:7

When I was a young Christian I had a difficult time finding the right words when I prayed. I asked the Lord to help me to speak fluently to Him. Soon I found my prayers flowing smoothly as I praised Him and poured out my request before Him. I also struggled when I needed to speak to a crowd of people. One time when I was searching for the right words to minister to a group I asked God to fill my thoughts and heart with the words He wanted me to say. The Lord spoke to my spirit and told me: *"Don't work at it so hard. Say what you mean and mean what you say. If a person really means what they say they will be speaking from their heart and they will say what they need to say. You are My child and your heart is good. Speak from your heart."* I have put this advice into practice many times since then and it always works. The words come out from my heart. It is in the heart where the Spirit of God lives. I allow God's Spirit to speak through me whether I verbally speak to a group or I write the words on a page to be read. I have learned to yield to the Spirit and allow Him to talk through me. When I do this, I don't struggle to find the right words to say.

> *"Let the words of my mouth and the meditation of my heart be acceptable in Your sight, O Lord, my strength and my Redeemer."* Psalm 19:14

I often recite Psalm 19:14 in prayer to God before I have to speak in front of people. I always want to speak only that which I am supposed to say and keep in mind that the main purpose I am speaking is to glorify God. If I speak from my heart with the Spirit of God as my leader the message I deliver will be that which He wants me to say. As a Christian, and as a leader in my church, it is a priority to me that I glorify God in all I say and do.

If you are jumbling your words when you talk to God, let go and relax. Don't try so hard. Speak through your spirit with your words and God will understand even if your words are mixed up. The more you practice talking to God the more fluent your words will flow. God already knows your need, He simply wants you to come to Him and tell Him what you need.

A prayer doesn't have to be a pretty prayer, just do the best you can and one day you will find the words come easier as you talk to God. That is what prayer is, it is simply talking to God. God understands us no matter what language we speak because He is our creator. And we understand God by reading His Word. We can pray right words by praying inline with God's Word. When you pray God's Word back to Him, He stands by His Word and He will see to it that it is done unto you according to your faith. He will never go against what He said in His Word. The more of His Word you get into you, the better you learn how to speak in line with it. Our words can get jumbled up sometimes but they will be words of wisdom, love and understanding when we get God's Word in us.

> *"And the prayer of faith will save the sick, and the Lord will raise him up. And if he has committed sins, he will be forgiven."* James 5:15

This verse in James five tells us that a prayer said in faith will heal the sick and sins will be forgiven. It does not say if the prayer has all of the right words or if it is said in the right order. It simply says, *if it is said in faith*. God doesn't answer our prayers that we say according to any rules that man have set up. If you have faith and believe and speak in line with God's Word when you pray, then God will answer. So relax, have faith, and pray. God hears you and He understands.

> *"Therefore I say to you, whatever things you ask when you pray, believe that you*

receive them, and you will have them." Mark 11:24

"And whatever things you ask in prayer, believing, you will receive." Matthew 21:22

Heavenly Father,

Thank You for Your Word that guides and directs me. Thank You that I can learn how to talk by speaking in agreement with Your Word. It is reassuring to know that You understand me even when my words get out of order. I am so blessed that You love me so much that You lean down your ear to hear my prayers. Help me keep Your Word in my heart and in my thoughts, that I will speak from my spirit with words of understanding and love.

In Jesus' name
Amen

"Ask, and it will be given to you; seek, and you will find; knock, and it will be opened to you." Matthew 7:7

Printed in the United States
By Bookmasters